Mali Conflict of 20_

Tchioffo Kodjo

Mali Conflict of 2012-2013: A Critical Assessment

Patterns of Local, Regional and Global Conflict and Resolution Dynamics in Post-colonial and Post-cold war Africa

LAP LAMBERT Academic Publishing

Impressum / Imprint

Bibliografische Information der Deutschen Nationalbibliothek: Die Deutsche Nationalbibliothek verzeichnet diese Publikation in der Deutschen Nationalbibliografie; detaillierte bibliografische Daten sind im Internet über http://dnb.d-nb.de abrufbar.

Alle in diesem Buch genannten Marken und Produktnamen unterliegen warenzeichen-, marken- oder patentrechtlichem Schutz bzw. sind Warenzeichen oder eingetragene Warenzeichen der jeweiligen Inhaber. Die Wiedergabe von Marken, Produktnamen, Gebrauchsnamen, Handelsnamen, Warenbezeichnungen u.s.w. in diesem Werk berechtigt auch ohne besondere Kennzeichnung nicht zu der Annahme, dass solche Namen im Sinne der Warenzeichen- und Markenschutzgesetzgebung als frei zu betrachten wären und daher von jedermann benutzt werden dürften.

Bibliographic information published by the Deutsche Nationalbibliothek: The Deutsche Nationalbibliothek lists this publication in the Deutsche Nationalbibliografie; detailed bibliographic data are available in the Internet at http://dnb.d-nb.de.

Any brand names and product names mentioned in this book are subject to trademark, brand or patent protection and are trademarks or registered trademarks of their respective holders. The use of brand names, product names, common names, trade names, product descriptions etc. even without a particular marking in this work is in no way to be construed to mean that such names may be regarded as unrestricted in respect of trademark and brand protection legislation and could thus be used by anyone.

Coverbild / Cover image: www.ingimage.com

Verlag / Publisher:
LAP LAMBERT Academic Publishing
ist ein Imprint der / is a trademark of
OmniScriptum GmbH & Co. KG
Heinrich-Böcking-Str. 6-8, 66121 Saarbrücken, Deutschland / Germany
Email: info@lap-publishing.com

Herstellung: siehe letzte Seite /
Printed at: see last page
ISBN: 978-3-659-45699-2

Zugl. / Approved by: Addis Ababa, University of Leipzig and University of Addis Ababa, Diss., 2014

Synopsis

This book incepts from the empirical evidence that, far from being an isolated predicament, Mali conflict of 2012 and 2013 is part and parcel of a dynamic system of crises which lacerate the country since its independence. From a global perspective, it investigates the 2012 and 2013 Mali security crisis and the patterns of its resolution using post-colonial and post-cold war lenses in the context of recurring crises in the country. Using a combination of Critical Discourse Analysis, Critical Terrorism Studies and Strategic Conflict Assessment, the research identifies and disentangles various and often self-reinforcing aspects of Mali conflict. Then, it unravels the overlapping bilateral, regional and global arrangements established in order to restore peace and stability in the country. To channel the analysis, Mali conflict is captured through the lens of a post-colonial and post-cold war francophone African nation-state building process in the context of new regionalism, fluid translocal terrorism and transnational organized crimes. At the height of Mali crisis, extreme fragmentation of political elites intertwined in a spatial north-south dichotomy is symptomatic of a post-colonial 'belly' and 'phallus' democracy. In addition, international donors' strategic complacency embedded in a sheer 'dead aid' political economy fuels the dialectic of creed, greed and grievance. Yet, international intervention in the country is designed mainly around post-colonial bilateral ties colluding and conflicting structurally with sub-regional, regional and global arrangements to solve the conflict. These peacekeeping arrangements evolve in a cooperation/competition logic embedded in power-play strategies haunted by the fantasy of the burden sharing doctrine.

Table of Contents

List of Tables and Figures

List of Abbreviations and Acronyms

A

ACIRC
  African Capacity for Immediate Response to Crises ·
  99
AFISMA
  African-led International Support Mission to Mali ·
  12, 69, 70, 72, 78, 93, 94, 97, 98, 99, 100, 101,
  102, 103, 105, 107, 110, 111, 115, 116
ANAD
  Agreement of the Protocol on Non-Aggression and
  Assistance in Defence of ECOWAS · 37
ANSAR Dine
  "helpers of the (Islamic) religion" or "defenders of the
  faith" in Arabic · 11
APSA
  African Peace and Security Architecture · 12, 34, 38,
  39, 77, 78, 83, 85, 89, 93, 98, 99, 102, 104, 105,
  115, 116
AQIM
  Al-Qaeda in the Islamic Maghreb · 40, 44, 46, 47, 48,
  49, 53, 54, 55, 56, 57, 61, 63, 69, 88, 90, 91, 92, 93
AQMI
  al-Qaeda in the Islamic Maghreb · 11, 46, 54, 56, 93
ASF
  African Standby Force · 99
ATT
  Amadou Toumani Touré · 50, 57, 58, 59, 60, 61, 63,
  64, 65, 68, 76, 79, 80, 81, 85, 87, 90, 93, 94, 100
AU
  African Union · 10, 12, 16, 34, 38, 39, 48, 66, 73, 77,
  78, 79, 80, 81, 82, 83, 84, 85, 88, 89, 92, 94, 95, 97,
  98, 99, 100, 101, 102, 103, 104, 105, 106, 107,
  114, 115, 116

C

CDA
  Critical Discourse Analysis · 15, 18, 19, 20
CEAO
  West African Economic Community · 36, 37
CFR
  Council on Foreign Relations · 16
CONOPS
  Concept of Operations · 101
CRISE
  Centre for Research on Inequality, Human Security
  and Ethnicity · 30
CTS
  Critical Terrorism Studies · 18, 20, 21

D

DFID
  UK Department For International Development · 15,
  22

E

ECOWAS
  Economic Community of West African States · 7, 10,
  12, 16, 34, 37, 48, 63, 64, 65, 66, 73, 77, 78, 79, 80,
  81, 82, 83, 84, 85, 86, 87, 88, 89, 90, 91, 92, 93, 94,
  95, 96, 97, 98, 100, 101, 102, 103, 105, 106, 107,
  111, 114, 115, 116
EU
  European Union · 14, 16, 34, 66, 69
EUTM-Mali
  European Union Training Mission in Mali · 12, 34

F

FP
  Foreign Policy · 16

G

GRIP
  Groupe de Recherche et d'Information sur la Paix et
  la Sécurité · 16

H

HI
  Horizontal Inequality · 31
HRW
  Human Right Watch · 16

I

ICG
  International Crisis Group · 16, 64, 70, 72, 84, 85, 86,
  87, 88, 95, 96, 98, 104
IMF
  International Monetary Fund · 25
ISS
  Institute for Security Studies · 16, 48, 49

4

Chap I. Introduction and Overview

Sporadic terrorist attacks are now part of the daily routine of Malians. Yet, May 2014 clashes in Kidal carried back Mali conflict to the forefront of global newspapers and media headlines[1]. The complexity of the political and security crisis facing the country was again exposed when the Prime Minister Moussa Mara and his delegation were attacked during his visit to Kidal governorate on 17 May 2014 by MNLA separatists leading to another debacle of the Malian army in the region. This is a clear illustration of the challenges facing Mali despite bilateral, regional and global endeavors to assist the country in order to restore the state authority over its territory.

From this observation, this book investigates how Mali, an African nation-state in the post- colonial and post-cold war era ensures its security in a global milieu. From this broad inquiry, subsequent interrogations are deducted specifically which kind of crises Mali is confronted to and how these crises are addressed by the country and its partners in a global perspective. In order to fix the analysis in suitable spatial-temporal context, this book investigates Mali crises and subsequent responses during 2012 and 2013, years of rich dynamics and crisis climax across the country.

At the height of Mali crisis between 2012 and 2013, a swift succession of events transmuted an initial nationalist secessionist rebellion into a regional jihadist movement claiming beyond Mali, the whole western Africa[2]. The fragility and collapse of the Malian state during that period and the involvement of bilateral,

---

[1] Heavy fights between Malian government and MNLA rebels broke out on 17 May 2014 more than six months after Mali was supposedly stepping out of a complex crisis that threaten to split it.

[2] MUJAO is the Movement for Oneness and Jihad in West Africa. It was formed in 2011 with the ideal to spread Jihad across West Africa. CNN article 'Battling al-Qaeda in Africa' gives details about the career of MUJAO leader Mokhtar Belmokhtar. See more at http://www.bbc.com/news/world-us-canada-23796920, accessed March 2014.

regional and global actors in the crisis resolution process added complexity to the crisis.

This book critically examines the patterns and dynamics of Mali crisis at its height embedded in its local, regional and global dimensions. It further disentangles and dissects the overlapping conflicts and the resolution patterns dynamics at the local, bilateral, sub-regional, continental and multilateral levels.

The book uses both primary and secondary sources and draws heavily on official documents such as reports, decisions and policy instruments of the ECOWAS, African Union, European Union and the United Nations. Information from bilateral arrangements between Mali and France as well as between Mali and the USA are from crucial importance. This research also makes an extensive usage of information gathered in academic books, journal and think-thank articles. All this is supplemented by details gained through personal observation and involvement in some summits and conferences relevant to investigate and analyze Mali crisis dynamics at its height between 2012 and 2013.

I.1. Background of the study

The protracted crisis of 2012-2013 in Mali is at best captured through the lens of post-colonial Africa nation-building process in the context of Africa's new regionalism, systemic cross-border terrorism and transnational organized crimes. It is also investigated by a scrupulous assessment of various overlapping conflict resolution arrangements and their intricate dynamics.

Mali as a nation-state is France colonial construction. The country gained its independence from France on 20 June 1960 as Federation of Mali. The World

Bank estimates its population to be 14.85 million people in 2012 composed of more than twenty ethnic groups, including the Bambara, Malinke, Dogon, Fulani, Songhai, Moors and Touareg[3]. Geographically, the country is strategically located at the heart of West Africa straddling between the Sahara desert and the Sahel region. Landlocked, the country is crossed from south to north by the Niger River, 4200 km long which is the principal river of West Africa and most important water resource of Mali[4]. The country's official language is French and the religious landscape is dominated by Muslims (90%) as stated by the Population Reference Bureau[5]. The remainder consists of Christians. But it is important to recall that like the rest of the continent, religious practices in Mali are more often tinted with African traditional beliefs and practices.

The post-colonial African nation-building process has been complicated by autocratic political regimes inherited from the colonial administration and mixed with ethnic rivalries. In Provisional Notes on the Postcolony (1992), Mbembe esteems that in Post-colonial Africa, 'power is exercised with a degree of violence and naked exploitation that has its antecedents in previous colonial regimes' (p 36)[6]. Mali follows this pattern because eight years after its independence, a military coup overthrown the regime of Modibo Keita and the

---

[3] The World Bank provides comprehensive data about Mali economic performance. See more at http://www.banquemondiale.org/fr/country/mali, accessed March 2014.

[4] Akinlawon Ladipo Mabogunje recalls that the Niger is also called Joliba in its upper course. For more details about the article, see Encyclopædia Britannica article 'the Niger River' at http://www.britannica.com/EBchecked/topic/414815/Niger-River, accessed March 2014.

[5] The Population Reference Bureau suggests that Muslim population is likely to increase in sub-Saharan Africa due to high fertility rates. Mali total fertility rate is 5.6 Children per women according to the PRB. For more details, see the article 'Évolution démographiques des pays musulmans' by Farzaneh Roudi-Fahimi, John F. May and Allyson C. Lynch at http://www.prb.org/FrenchContent/2013/demographics-muslims-fr.aspx, accessed March 2014.

[6] Achille Mbembe is an authority in the field of Post-colonial francophone Africa. For details, see his seminal article "Provisional Notes on the Postcolony" published by the Journal of the International African Institute, Vol. 62, No. 1, (1992), pp. 3-37.

country sank into twenty-two (22) years of brutal dictatorship of Moussa Traore. After the demise of Moussa Traore in 1991 and the instauration of a multiparty system, the country was painted as a thriving democracy during the successive regime of Alpha Oumar Konaré and Amadou Toumani Touré (Joe Penney, 2013)[7].

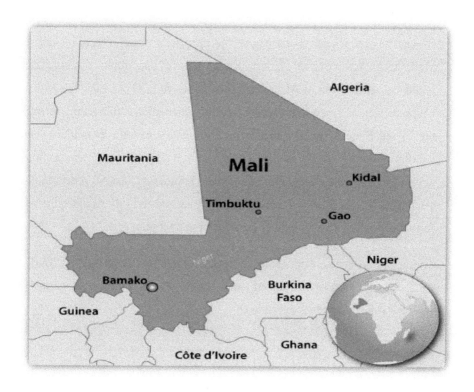

Figure 1 - A map of Mali that positions the country in West Africa and highlights the main cities as well the strategic importance of the River Niger

However, this simplistic depiction of Mali as a blossoming democracy hits its limits when the degree of governance decay was publicly exposed by the

---

[7] Joe Penney (2013) suggests that Mali is a low standard democracy built on sand. See more in the article 'Mali's Model Democracy Myth' in ThinkAfricaPress at http://thinkafricapress.com/mali/restoring-democracy-mali-never-had, accessed March 2014.

convoluted predicaments of 2012-2013 crises. The crisis reopens the debate on multiparty election as a natural guarantee for a successful democracy (Joe Penney, 2013). Conversely, Mali, on the brink of splitting, has to look for its partners to help resolve the conflicts and restore the state authority over its territory.

A natural approach in post-colonial Africa entails seeking assistance of former colonial master whenever the country security is at stake. The originality of Mali's tactic in a post-cold war era, was to seek for opportunities of assistance within the region from its African 'brothers' through ECOWAS and the African Union as well as to explore support from the international community through the United Nations system and the European Union to train its military. This conflict resolution pattern and its dynamics are the upshot of bilateral military agreements with the former colonial power (France), ECOWAS peacekeeping arrangement embedded in the broader AU Peace and Security Architecture and further embroiled with global UN peacekeeping doctrines.

These arrangements, their 'hidden' agendas, and their overlapping conflict resolution mechanisms coupled with their hefty bureaucracies added sophistication to the crisis resolution.

I.2. Objectives of the study and Research Gaps

The general objective of this book is to provide critical insights on the complex origins and key divers of Mali crisis and to untie the overlapping conflict resolution mechanisms and the dynamics of various actors involved into the conflict at its height between 2012 and 2013.

Specifically, the essay aims to:

- dissect the anatomy of the crisis settings and the structural background of its drivers rooted in Mali geostrategic position in the region between the Sahara desert and semi-arid Sahel, favorable field for smuggling, terrorism and transnational organized crimes ; The background of this multi-faceted crisis is also analyzed in the circumstances of Mali political shortcomings and its ramifications mostly through an acute governance crisis; The Touareg question manifested in MNLA and MAA secessionism provides another angle of reflection on the crisis blips; The crisis must be decisively analyzed through ANSAR Dine, AQMI, MUJAO and other Islamic jihadists groups challenges deep-seated on wider regional-global terrorism challenges.

  o examine the military putsch and the tenuous path towards the restoration of the constitutional order; The internal rivalries and split of the Malian army provides an objective lens to assess the military putsch and its driving grievances; On the other hand, the swift progression of the rebels southward and the unilateral proclamation of the independence of [8] is scrutinized through MNLA alliance with Islamic jihadist groups in addition to the failure of the state in the North; the short-lived independence of AZAWAD is assessed through division between the MNLA and Islamic jihadists groups over the new country ideology as well as the unanimous condemnation of Mali partial split by all key regional and global players; the tenuous path to the restoration of constitutional order coupled with the power struggle within transitional institutions is gauged through the heterogeneity of the interim government along with hidden agenda of political and military leaders; the decisive signing of Ouagadougou agreements

---

[8] AZAWAD means 'land of transhumance' in Tamasheq, the Touareg language.

as well as the organization of presidential election is evaluated within ECOWAS/AU and France mediation in the crisis.

☛ disentangle bilateral, regional and global arrangements towards the restoration of Malian state authority over its entire territory; the failure of MICEMA and the stalemate in the establishment of AFISMA provides insight to analyze APSA challenges especially on the relationship between African Union and the RECs, specifically ECOWAS in the absence of a central leadership in Bamako; the swift intervention of France with the launch of operation Serval is investigated through the protection of vital economic interests as well as global powers competition for spheres of influence in the region; the establishment of MINUSMA to take over AFISMA is another point of inquiry on the relationship between the UN and regional arrangements specially the African Union when it comes to peacekeeping on the continent; The European Union launch of EUTM-Mali, officially in order to train the defeated Malian army is analyzed beyond simplistic international assistance to support the country but rather through France momentum driven by continued battle for sphere of influence and preservation of economic interests in the region.

The book contributes to fill the gap of pertinent assessments of the conflict at its peak between 2012 and 2013 which take into account the entanglement of international interventions combined to the multiple intertwined and self-reinforcing dimensions of the crisis specifically the acute governance crisis, the grievances in the north disheveled in a transnational terrorism agenda.

I.3. Research Hypothesis

The research proposition guiding the book is that the Malian turmoil is a complex mixture of cumulated historic grievances, poor governance and failure of international aid. And without carefully unpacking the different dimensions of the crisis, approaches to resolve the conflict would end up operating in isolation yielding sup-optimal outcomes at best or postpone an inevitable collapse of the Malian state at worst.

This hypothesis and the relationship between its variables are grounded in the review of literature. The research will consistently test it on the backdrop of Mali experience in order to account for the spectrum of explanations that could justify the crisis and the dynamics of resolution mechanisms.

I.IV. Scope and limitations of the Study

The crisis commencement can be traced back few years earlier with the spillover of 2011 military intervention in Libya and the start of Touareg rebellion. While this book acknowledges and assesses the key drivers of the crisis, they are by no mean the central object of this paper. Furthermore, the crisis has persisted beyond 2013 as attested by May 2014 events in Kidal. This is also not the focus of this essay.

The spatial scope of the book pinpoints Mali in the wide open spaces of the Sahelo-Saharan region intertwined in the western African and broader continental landscape. This space is also the milieu of transnational organized crimes and other smuggling activities which are beyond the scope of this book. However, their impact in the proliferation and sustainability of Islamic extremist networks in the area is assessed. Additionally, the involvement of global actors such as France, US, EU and UN are crucial to understand the dynamics put in place to answer the crisis.

In addition to English, the author speaks and writes fluently French, the official language of Mali. This provides an opportunity to dive into relevant scholarly, academic and journal articles written in the language.

The essay may also suffer specific bias in its analysis of the African Union involvements in the crisis since the author works for the organization and some of the expertise provided during the book writing was made by professionals from the institution.

I.V. Research Material and Sources

Quality of scholarly work is deeply tributary of the significance and insights provided by the research material and academic sources used to produce knowledge.

In the course of academic sources gathering, a list of criteria was applied to identify and select relevant material. The research made sure that the material is: (1) authoritative in the sense of the expertise of the editor and its academic credentials; (2) the systematic usage and citation of credible sources as well as the presence of a reference list or bibliography; (3) the writings are substantially peer-reviewed and checked for accuracy; (4) the level of bias of the author is minor to ensure that the debate stays fundamentally impartial.

Non-academic sources addressing the topic were also given due consideration and weighted vis-à-vis the arguments provided. Specifically, key actors and institutions communiqués, speeches, reports and interviews were given due consideration. Also, newspaper article with credible information were taken into account. The research then organized this considerable amount of relevant information into categories in order to facilitate its exploitation. Research material was organized in the following categories: academic sources, institutional sources and internet sources.

I.V.1. Academic Sources

This category comprises academic books, academic journals scholarly and articles that provide the theoretical background as well as in-depth insights on the crisis in Mali.

On the theoretical framework, 'The Archeology of Knowledge' of Michel Foucault offers a brilliant primer on text analysis to exhume hidden connection between what is said, written and the magnitude of its impact on the way people live. Another wonderful theoretical material is the book 'Dissemination' by Jacques Derrida, father of deconstructionism who insightfully insufflates that academic writings must be carefully dissected in order to detect all possible implied and hidden perspectives. Specifically, 'The Dialectics of Discourse' of Norman Fairclough provides specific insights on Critical Discourse Analysis (CDA).

In a more technical perspective, *'Critical Terrorism Studies: A New Research Agenda' of* Richard Jackson, Marie Breen Smyth and Jeroen Gunning provide a strong approach to Critical Terrorism Studies. The handbook on 'Conducting Conflict Assessments: Guidance Notes' of DFID assists to make the best use of Strategic Conflict Assessment in regard to this book topic.

These authors' arguments and technics are appraised in the methodology section of the book.

I.V.2. Institutional sources

Institutional sources considered comprise international organizations, think-thanks, NGOs as well as governments material pouring out variety of official papers and analyses addressing the crisis in Mali.

ECOWAS, AU, EU and UN are the key international organizations which provided strategic reports as well as press release and communiqués at the height of Mali crisis. Significant governmental insights and agendas is extracted from documents of foreign ministries of the region's country as well have key external powers which have vested interests in the crisis and geostrategic interests in the region.

The Council on Foreign Relations (CFR), the International Crisis Group (ICG), Foreign Policy (FP), Africa Center for Strategic Studies (ACSS), the Réseau de Recherche sur les Opérations de Paix (ROP), the Groupe de Recherche et d'Information sur la Paix et la Sécurité (GRIP) and the Institute for Security Studies (ISS) are some of the main think-thanks which extensively analyzed the crisis in Mali and produced relevant research findings. Reports from NGOs like Human Right Watch (HRW) were also used to gather specific data.

I.V.3. Internet sources

At first sight, it is not advisable to exploit internet material for the purpose of academic knowledge production. However, current trends in information gathering as well as the growing usage of blogs and Facebook groups have

16

contributed to leverage the acceptance of these tools as support for valid literature. Still, a careful analysis and evaluation of the argument and the bias of the authors must be effectively taken into account.

For the purpose of this book, specific newspaper articles and blogs articles were considered credible to deliver critical insights on the evolution and the perception of the crisis at different levels. Based on the criteria cited above for knowledge production in academic milieu and in accordance with their specific focus on Mali, the writers and analysts selected include Bruce Whitehouse, Gregory Mann, Bruce Hall, Bazz Lecocq, Isaline Bergamaschi, Paul D. Williams, Priscilla Sadatchy, Steven Zyck, Robert Muggaht, Roland Marchal, Remi Carayol, Mark Levine, Boubacar Yalkoué, Lorie-Anne Benoni and Laurent Touchard.

The originality of these analysts resides in the eminence of their background as scholars, international recognized journalists and their crucial specialization in the region geostrategic issues. Some of them write their own blogs like Bruce Whitehouse who is the author of the well-known 'Bridges from Bamako'[9]. Other blogs intensely writing on the Mali crisis include 'The Moor Next Door' who consistently provided delved understandings of Mali crisis. Traditional print and online Newspapers which ardently poured out articles on Mali crisis comprise Le monde diplomatique, Slate Afrique, Jeune Afrique, Reuters, Mali Web, Xinhua, Deutsche Welle, The Guardian, Al-Jazeera, France24 and the New York Times.

---

[9] Bruce Whitehuse is a professor of anthropology at Lehigh University in Pennsylvania. He is interested on Mali and especially Bamako that he labels a 'budding metropolis'. See more on his insightful blog at http://bridgesfrombamako.com/, accessed March 2014.

I.VI. Methodology of the Research

Scholarly debate about the 'right method' is a sea snake reoccurring consistently in the academic milieu. Moving beyond this sterile knot, this book considers methods as guidance and leverage tools to use in order to produce scientifically credible knowledge. Therefore, the study makes use of a combination of methods, trying to harness the best of their potentials for the benefit of the analysis and knowledge production in the perspective of the topic under investigation.

After careful consideration and deep exploration, Critical Discourse Analysis (CDA), Strategic Conflict Assessment (SCA) coupled at the core with Critical Terrorism Studies (CTS) provide strategic guidance to assess the crisis in Mali during the years 2012 and 2013.

I.VI.1. Critical Discourse Analysis (CDA)

The Foundation of Qualitative Research in Education postulates that critical discourse analysis "is not an effort to capture literal meanings; rather it is the investigation of what language does or what individuals or cultures accomplish through language"[10]. It goes on to state that CDA interrogates "how meaning is constructed, and how power functions in society"[11].

Thinkers like Michel Foucault or Jacques Derrida contributions to intellectual debate is a skillful mix of sophisticated works fundamental to critical thinking.

---

[10] The Foundation of Qualitative Research in Education is founded by Harvard University to provide reference knowledge on qualitative methods and researches. See its article 'Discourse Analysis' at http://isites.harvard.edu/icb/icb.do?keyword=qualitative&pageid=icb.page340345, accessed March 2014.
[11] Ibid.

In *The Archeology of Knowledge* (1972), Foucault (1972, p 27) holds that discourse produces power through framing, arrangement and categorization of knowledge production. In this vein, he asks: "according to what rules has a particular statement been made, and consequently according to what rules could other similar statements be made?"[12] . Foucauldian Discourse Analysis pertinent questioning and influential reflection model on discourse and power interrelations have gain a significant foothold in the academic milieu and serves as a decisive approach in acute analysis.

Jacques Derrida coined the term deconstruction which then became a key concept in critical thinking jargon. Derrida deconstruction is based on the argument that discourse must be understood beyond the set of well-formed sentences; rather it must be undone methodically to find its concealed meaning. In Dissemination, Derrida (1983, p 63) translated by Barbara Johnson ably pinpoints that "a text is not a text unless it hides from the first comer, from the first glance, the law of its composition and the rules of its game"[13]. Jacques Derrida's school of deconstructionism has inspired generations of scholars and thinkers and its assets contribute to snoop deeply into relevant research material.

Professor Norman Fairclough is presented as one of the pioneer to distinctively write on CDA regarding social and linguistic issues. In his book *Critical Discourse Analysis: The Critical Study of Language*, Fairclough examines on one hand the language in relation to ideology and power and on the other language as a site of dynamic social and cultural change within society. He posits that four steps drive a CDA: (1) discover social hitches by identifying the signification of signs and textual symbols (semiotic); (2) determine the

---

[12] M. Foucault. *The Archeology of Knowledge,* London: Routledge, 1972, p 27.

[13] Jacques Derrida, Barbara Johnson (translation). *Dissemination*, University of Chicago Press, 1983, p 63.

difficulties to address the hitches; (3) assess if the hitches reinforce or weaken the social order; (4) isolate and evaluate possible way forward[14].

As Fairclough (2012) established, CDA is a trans-disciplinary approach which dialogues "with other disciplines and methods addressing contemporary processes of social change". That is the case of Critical Terrorism Studies (CTS).

I.VI.2. Critical Terrorism Studies (CTS)

Mali protracted crisis is embedded in a global dynamic of terrorism and transnational organized crime. Emerging after the 9/11 terror attacks, CTS intends to move beyond the orthodox or classical terrorism studies which simplistically put state at the heart its analysis. CTS accuses orthodox terrorism studies to be state-centric and therefore failing to ask relevant questions namely on the drivers, triggers and process of generation of terrorism, the assessment of terror nature and production as well as the origin of this terror beyond the one-dimensional conception excluding states actors as potential terrorists.

In *Critical Terrorism Studies: A New Research Agenda,* Richard Jackson, Marie Breen Smyth and Jeroen Gunning widen the scope of terrorism studies by proposing an innovative approach which pushes that "more research needs to be done in a multidisciplinary fashion to deepen existing knowledge and to push the envelope in new directions. More research needs to be collated about the multivariate cause of terrorism [and] to explore the issue of radicalization

---

[14] See Norman Fairclough article on Critical Discourse Analysis (2012) at
https://www.academia.edu/3791325/Critical_discourse_analysis_2012_, accessed March 2014.

leading to terrorism [...] the connection to the preventive strands of countering radicalization [...] and the hard effects of counterterrorism efforts"(2009)[15].

Based on the predicament that constructive 'disagreements among experts are the driving force of the scientific enterprise' (Ranstorp, 2009, p 17)[16], CTS believes with Charlotte Heath-Kellya, Lee Jarvisb and Christopher Baker-Beallc that orthodox terrorism studies focus on "interpreting *[the international]*[17] as an abstract field composed of state-units and international organisations, rather than constituted through multiple lives and domains of experience" has "overly formalized" and limit its enquiry. The scholars argue in favor of the inclusion of empirical and personal experience to build more critical analysis of terrorism and counterterrorism (Heath-Kellya, Jarvisb, Baker-Beallc, 2009).

Asymmetrical threats and conflicts are equally at the midpoint of CTS which seeks to expand the scope of terrorism studies to investigate the dynamics of novel conflicts where a classic state army will not confront another state's army but an insurgency coupled to a transnational terrorist movement. CTS can provide significant help on how to investigate the situation in northern Mali per se where terrorism and armed conflict seems to overlap.

I.VI.3. Strategic Conflict Assessment (SCA)

Strategic Conflict Assessment refers to the method of conflict investigation initially designed by Jonathan Goodhand, Tony Vaux and Robert Walke for

---

[15] Richard Jackson, Marie Breen Smyth, Jeroen Gunning. Critical Terrorism Studies: A New Research Agenda, Routledge, 2009, p.32.

[16] Marc Sageman cited by Magnus Ranstorp (contributor) in Critical Terrorism Studies: A New Research Agenda, Routledge, 2009, p.17.

[17] Emphasis added by the author.

DFID[18]. It aims to provide international organizations, NGOs as well as bilateral and multilateral development agencies with the best tools to "analyse conflict; better assess conflict related risks associated with development or humanitarian assistance; and develop options for more conflict sensitive policies and programmes" (Goodhand et al., 2002, p 4).

SCA comparative advantage is its practical utility tracing clearly the path to follow to analyze a conflict with an emphasis on the analysis of international responses to the conflict. It fits particularly well in assessing the Malian crisis where a complex set of bilateral, regional and global actors intervened with the common overlapping objective of resorbing the crisis facing the country.

In a deep-seated crisis like the Malian one where contention is profoundly intertwined with creed, greed, grievances, stereotypes and political agendas, SCA offers a flexible methodology which "adapt[s] according to the needs and objectives of the end user [and] develop according to the nature and phase of the conflict;" (Goodhand et al., 2002, p 7). Accordingly, in this book, SCA will be molded to suit academic writing and produce scholarly valid work.

To apply the SCA technique, it is capital to systematically examine the structural sources of vulnerability, the key actors and agendas and finally the dynamics of the conflict using a multidisciplinary approach.

---

[18] DFID. Conducting Conflict Assessments – Guidance Notes, 2002, DFID London.

Chap II. Review of Literature and Theoretical Framework

I. On Post-colonial and Post-cold War Nation-State building in Africa

The body of literature on post-colonial nation state building in Africa is rich. This section examines academic literature on post-colonial nation-state building in Africa and its dynamics in the post-cold war era.

Achille Mbembe points out that, "the notion [of] 'postcolony' identifies specifically a given historical trajectory - that of societies recently emerging from the experience of colonization and the violence which the colonial relationship, par *excellence*, involves"(1992, p.1). In *Provisional Notes on the Postcolony*, Mbembe deconstructs the post-colony in what he calls the 'obscene' and the 'grotesque', manifestation of a 'theatrical' self-seeking milieu where 'shamelessness', physical and verbal abuses drive a narrow-minded society limited to its mouth, belly and phallus. He continues on this line, stating that state achievements in post-colonial Africa is meager in opposite to its tendency towards 'ceremonial' and 'exhibitionism'. Furthermore, he questions the population tolerance and collusion with the system, "even, with violence and domination in its most heady form" (Mbembe, 1992, p.17). Mbembe harsh criticism of the post-colonial society culminates and drives discussion on nation-state building when he insists that "the postcolony is chaotically pluralistic, yet it has nonetheless an internal coherence" (1992, p.1).

Scholarly debates on nation-state building in Africa take multiple directions. However, there is a need to elucidate the very notion of nation-state before diving into its construction in post-colonial and post-cold war Africa.

The theory of nation-state encompasses the notion of nation and state and their interdependence. The concept of nation is diversely apprehended and understood. Ernest Renan expounds a nation as a moral conscience which seeks its legitimacy from the "subordination of the individual to the communal good" (Renan, 1882)[19]. In 'Imagined communities: reflections on the origin and spread of nationalism', Benedict Anderson prescribes that nation are imagined communities in the sense that "regardless of the actual inequality and exploitation that may prevail in each, the nation   is always conceived as a deep, horizontal comradeship" (1991, p.50). Anderson argues that nations do not exist and are merely the fruit of discursive socio-constructed communities where most people do not know each other but "yet in the minds of each lives the image of their communion" (1991, p.49). While this theoretical contention is not the direct object of this paper, the concept of nation provides substance for this paper when its value bring about the historical as well as the socio-cultural sharing of a common identity. It is used specifically to investigate Tuareg claims of AZAWAD as their nation.

Max Weber classical definition of a state is that of "a human community that claims the monopoly of the legitimate use of physical force within a given territory" (1946, p.48)[20].   Tilly (1975) argues that '[a]n organization which controls the population occupying a defined territory is a state in so far as (1) it is differentiated from other organizations operating in the same territory; (2) it is

---

[19] Ernest Renan, "What is a Nation?", text of a conference delivered at the Sorbonne on March 11th, 1882, in Ernest Renan, Qu'est-ce qu'une nation?, Paris, Presses-Pocket, 1992. (translated by Ethan Rundell).

[20] Weber, Max. "Politics as a Vocation," in Gerth and Mills. From Max Weber. New York, 1946. P 48.

24

autonomous; (3) it is centralized; and (4) its divisions are formally coordinated with one another'.

These definitions stress the structural and organizational aspects of the state without mentioning state functions (apart from the monopoly of violence in Weber's definition). However, both focus very much on the importance of a centralized form of authority. For Weber in particular, the ideal type modern state is underpinned by a 'rational-legal' bureaucracy.

Michael Mann (1994) adds another important dimension to the concept of the state in his elaboration on 'infrastructural' power. Infrastructural power refers to the actual penetration of societies by state bureaucracies and state-sponsored programmes, such as public education, and the ability to enforce policy throughout the state's entire territory (Mann, 1994).

A range of typologies is available distinguishing among different aspects and fundamental forms of the state. These tend to characterize the state in terms of a specific dimension, be this political economy or scope. For instance the classification of the IMF or World Bank focuses on specific economic aggregates[21]. Other classifications focus on internal and external strengths as well as the specific orientation of a particular state. This is the case of fragile, failed and developmental states.

Many states in the developing world, in particular those in conflict or emerging from a crisis are often identified as fragile because they fail to meet many of the basic criteria highlighted by Weber, Tilly and Mann. These kinds of states tend to have only tenuous control of their population beyond the center, and their infrastructural capacity as well as the presence of state bureaucracy and services

---

[21] Seethe World Bank classifixcation at http://data.worldbank.org/, accessed March 2014.

is often minimal, up to the point where the quality of being a state becomes questionable (Herbst, 2000).

Robert Rotberg (2003) seeks to establish the root causes leading to nation-state collapse and a clear distinction between collapsed, failed and weak or fragile states. He posits that nation-state failure is a man-made process which starts by weakening the basic foundation of the state and culminate in its complete failure and collapse (Rotberg, 2003). He adds that pinpointing the root causes of a state failure is a challenging undertaking because 'research on failed states is insufficiently advanced for precise tipping points to be provided' (Rotberg, 2003, p.22). Yet, Rotberg (2003) argues that the spiral leading to state failure can be meticulously assessed by taking in account three warning indicators namely (1) the income and living standards, (2) the quality of leadership and (3) the level of violence and national human security rate.

However, Uchenna (2012) contends that in post-colonial Africa, the warning indicators of Rotberg alone cannot justify nation-state failure but can be primarily seen as the 'pivotal dimensions of policy learning' (p.41). He defends that complexity theory offers a more viable epistemological foundation of nation-state building in the continent moving beyond the linear and simplistic existing epistemology to seize the complexity of the phenomenon tangled in the cohabitation of different ethnicities and their capability to sustain a viable nation-state (Uchenna, 2012).

A truculent article of Amira Kheir (2010) shifts completely the focus and tries to explain 'why the nation-state is wrong for Africa'[22]. She argues that the dilemma of Africa statehood is not a crisis of capability, rather a crisis of inheritance (Kheir, 2010). She claims that the importation of the nation-state

---

[22] See 'Why the nation-state is wrong for Africa' by Amira Kheir on Pambazuka at http://pambazuka.org/en/category/comment/61829, accessed April 2014.

model on the continent ' renders it illegitimate in the eyes of the masses comprised of minorities, as the nation-state carries the legacies of colonial administrative rule and exploitative occupation' (Kheir, 2010). She pursues that the appropriation of nation-state construction based on the European model has been flawed and problematic in African 'realities of multi ethnic, racial, religious and linguistic societies' (Kheir, 2010). Kheir (2010) thinks that nation-state in Africa is a 'fabricated toxic vacuum' which has undermined 'territorial authentication but also identity authentication and legitimate societal interactions', foundation of strong nation-state. She worries that the structural flaws of 'contrived nationalism' have now become embedded in the system 'while not immediately acknowledged as an obvious discrepancy'.

An article by Ulf Engel and Gorm Rye Olsen suggests that in the post-cold war era, nation-states have been 'demised' as 'the major regime of territorialisation' as the current phase of globalization processes unfolds (Engel and Olsen, 2010). They argue that African states have gradually lost their clout and that 'authority in Africa is increasingly exercised beyond the state 'in the course of 'de- and reterrorialisation' processes ongoing in the region (Engel and Olsen, 2010). For them, the Westphalian system of sovereign states is consistently challenged in post-cold war Africa by shifting perspectives on authority, sovereignty and territory (Engel and Olsen, 2010). Lastly, they propose a new research agenda against this background which will take into account a 'spatial dimension' conceptualized 'as a dialectic process of deteritorrialisation and reterritorialisation' in order 'to map the forces and resources of either making or un-making new spatial references of social order' in the continent (Engel and Olsen, 2010, p 11).

II. On Greed, Creed, Grievance in Civil War and the Rise of Terrorism

The inquiry of conflicts triggers in complex crises like in Mali requires to examine overall theoretical trends and contention in the academic milieu. It is palpable that Mali protracted conflict is tangled amid socio-economic as well as ethno-religious tensions. Fruitful research on greed, creed and grievance offers key theoretical insights on the ongoing debate in scholarship and contribute immensely to the explanation of civil war causes since the end of cold war.

The central hypothesis of greed-related arguments is that civil war emanates from vertical inequalities originating from economic opportunities exploited by 'rational actors' (Jakobsen, 2012); grievance-based arguments propose that horizontal inequalities provides pedigrees to civil conflicts initiated by 'deprived actors' (Jakobsen, 2012); creed theory postulates for specific type of grievance rooted in religious, civilizational and cultural 'clashes' (Huttington, 1993).

Paul Collier and Anke Hoefller seminal work on *Greed and Grievance in Civil War* is an econometric analysis of civil conflicts which concludes that 'opportunities for primary commodity predation cause conflict' (Collier and Hoeffler, 2000). For them, economic incentives and opportunity structures motivate rebellion which must be 'financially viable' (Collier and Hoeffler, 2000, p 13). They postulate that a rebellion must also be economically feasible and for that reason its revenues 'appear to be linked to the capture of resources' (Collier and Hoeffler, 2000, p 2). For them, a rebellion must discursively build grievances to maintain cohesion and motivation within its troops and also to masquerade its predation objectives (Collier and Hoeffler, 2000). In this sense, they point that 'greed-rebellions need to manufacture subjective grievance for military cohesion and may find an objective grievance an effective basis for

28

generating it' (Collier and Hoeffler, 2000, p 14). Later, they equally accept that 'greed and grievance can co-habit' but quickly downplay grievance by stating that in order for grievance-driven rebellion to survive it might perhaps turn into a 'greed-rebellion' for its sustainability (Collier and Hoeffler, 2000, p 14). They conclude that the greed model 'performs well' to drive and sustain a civil war while the 'best-performing grievance model has very low explanatory power' (Collier and Hoeffler, 2000, p 26).

Often cited in the literature and praised by the World Bank, the quantitative analysis of Collier and Hoeffler has also been widely criticized by its peers. For example David Keen criticized Collier's work stating that 'it offers an attractive and numerically derived oversimplification that gives us the illusion of having understood a complex world while allowing us to overlook a range of difficult issues' (Keen, 2012, p 758). Cited by Keen, Cramer argues that economic motivation and rationality is insufficient to assess human behavior and Nathan points out to the nature and character of mass violence ignored by Collier (Keen, 2012, p 759). For him, 'Collier's almost exclusive focus on rebels during wartime is unhelpful' and must shift to examine priorities and agenda of counter-insurgency actors (Keen, 2012, p 759). Keen sharp criticism of Collier's work climaxes when he suggests that Collier's influence stems mainly from the sometimes 'ill-founded' impression of 'newness' and its 'politically convenient' formulas (Keen, 2012).

The standard and perhaps most popular account of internal violence research suggest that it is driven by sufficient level of accumulated grievance (Collier and Hoeffler, 2000, p.17). Early works on internal violence suggests that it is powered by a frustration-aggression mechanism which claims 'the principle that anger functions as a drive' (Gurr, 1970, p 35). In *Why Men Rebel*, Robert Gurr is a key proponent of this grievance-based thesis. He posits that 'relative deprivation' fuels the 'impetus to violence' (Gurr, 1970). Gurr defines relative deprivation as 'perceived discrepancy between value expectations and value capabilities' and claims that it is a 'precondition of revolution' (Gurr, 1970, p 37). For him, 'the intensity and scope of relative deprivation' impacts the potential and the magnitude for collective violence (Gurr, 1970, p 30). Further, he inquires the rational utility of violence admitting that frustration-aggression is an emotive non-rational theory but it however provides that this irrational human behavior of 'relieving some of their discontent through violence' is a by-product of their accumulated frustrations (Gurr, 1970).

Frances Stewart, another acclaimed researcher is a proponent of grievance-based motivation as civil conflicts triggers. In *Horizontal inequalities as a cause of conflict: a review of CRISE findings*, she reveals that 'horizontal inequalities (HIs)' are key drivers of grievance generating rebellion. She writes that 'HIs are inequalities among groups of people who share a common identity' (Stewart, 2010, p 6) which are rooted in colonial practices of privileging some groups and/or regions. Further, she complains that 'post-colonial policies have done little to correct these inequalities' (Stewart, 2010, p 16). Working for the CRISE program, Stewart (2010) lists ten major findings of her research group:

(1) the probability of conflict is higher in areas with greater economic and social HIs;

(2) Conflict is more likely where political, economic and social HIs are consistent. Conflict is less likely when a particular group faces deprivation in one dimension and dominates in another;

(3) inclusive (or power-sharing) government tends to reduce the likelihood of conflict;

(4) citizenship can be an important source of political and economic exclusion;

(5) Unequal cultural recognition among groups is an additional motivation for conflict and cultural 'events' can trigger conflict;

(6) perceptions of HIs affect the likelihood of conflict;

(7) one reason high value natural resources can lead to conflict is that they create high HIs;

(8) the nature of the state is a pivotal factor in determining whether serious conflict erupts and persists;

(9) some HIs are very persistent, even lasting for centuries;

(10) International policies and statistics are too often blind to HIs, although national policies are often more progressive in this respect.

She further adds that HIs are a 'multidimensional concept' comprising economic, social, political and cultural dimensions (Stewart, 2010, p 7). She also elaborates that HIs differs from 'vertical' inequality' (VI) which measures disparity among individuals or households (not groups) and is often confined to income or consumption (Stewart, 2010, p 6). Later, Stewart concludes that HIs are a crucial driver of conflicts when its different constituencies are 'are consistent across dimensions' (Stewart, 2010, p 32).

Keen supports Stewart thesis and pinpoints that HIs arguments does not reject greed but interact with it in complex ways (Keen, 2012, p 757). For Keen, Stewart HI theory 'was able to form a better assessment *[than Collier VI]*[23] of the role of inequalities in generating conflict' (Keen, 2012, p 760). Keen conversely adds that the contrast between Collier and Stewart position is clear when the first excludes grievances and government actors whereas the latter underscores the importance of state and counter-insurgency in shaping of HIs among regional, ethnic or religious groups (Keen, 2012, p 760).

A particular type of grievance is religious or creed-based differences. Samuel Huttington's 'clash of civilizations' is one of the prominent attempt to draw a new pattern for conflicts causes in the post-cold war era. Responding to

---

[23] Emphasis added.

Fukuyama's "end of history", Huttington seminal work "The Clash of Civilizations?" was published in 1993 in the Foreign Affairs Magazine. There, he states that 'a civilization is a cultural entity' and further enlarges that civilization is 'the highest cultural grouping of people and the broadest level of cultural identity people have short of that which distinguishes humans from other species' (Huttington, 1993, p 24). Huttington thesis is that conflicts in the future will occur along the cultural fault lines separating civilizations (Huttington, 1993, p 25). For him, civilizations are separated by history, language, culture, tradition and most importantly religion (Huttington, 1993, p 25). He divides civilizations among eight sets namely: "Western, Confucian, Japanese, Islamic, Hindu, Slavic-Orthodox, Latin American and possibly African" (Huttington, 1993).

In its seminal article, he projected that in a post-cold war world where globalization intensifies contact among groups, civilization consciousness upturns and fuels animosity between different civilization and the rise of fundamentalism and extremism (Huttington, 1993, p 26). The paper was later expanded in a book entitled 'The Clash of Civilizations and the Remaking of World Order' which has been very influential and controversial in the academic as well as political milieus. In the book, he further emphasizes that the rejection of 'American creed' simply means the ends of western civilization challenged by other civilizations mostly Islamic (Huttington, 1996).

A harsh criticism of Huttington's clash of civilizations was formulated by the famous scholar of subaltern studies, Edward Said. In a truculent article untitled 'The Clash of Ignorance' and published in 'The Nation', Said meticulously deconstructs 'vague' Huttington thesis. Said complains about Huttington 'personification of enormous entities called "the West" and "Islam"' (Said, 2001). He further attacks Huttington, suggesting that 'downright ignorance' on 'internal dynamics and plurality of every civilization' or about major contest on 'the definition or interpretation of each culture' characterize the 'demagogic' clash of civilisations (Said, 2001). Said is much more troubled when he declares that Huttington is not more than an 'ideologist' who wishes to transform civilizations into 'shut-down, sealed off-entities' purged from human agency towards cross-exchange and peace (Said, 2001).

He further adds that the clash of civilizations is simply a 'gimmick' that 'may give momentary satisfaction but little self-knowledge or informed analysis' (Said, 2001). Later, Said completely rejects the clash of civilizations arguing that it is a 'futile' hypothesis that reformulates cold-war opposition into the 'West versus the rest' and particularly Islam and effortlessly generalize 'cultural assertions' (Said, 2001).

In contrast, a study by Indra de Soysa examines the merits of Huttington 'creed-related,' civilizational clashes and finds that 'creed–related conflicts seem to be more prevalent in highly homogenous religious settings, particularly within largely Islamic and Catholic countries' (Sosya, 2001, p 17). This study does not contradict Huttington but posits that 'if there is a clash of civilizations, it is much likely that it is political rather than civilizational' (Sosya, 2001, p17).

Another interesting piece of work is the study of Eric Neumayer and Thomas Plumper untitled 'International Terrorism and the Clash of Civilizations'. Derived from Huttington's clash of civilisations, Neumayer and Plumper shift the focus and investigate 'patterns of inter-civilizational terrorism' (2009). They contends that terrorist leaders are 'rational' actors aiming for 'political influence in their country or wider region' and attack western foreign targets only to secure 'media and public attention' independently of the 'civilizational affiliation of either the terrorists or their victims' (Neumayer and Plumper, 2009, p 720). They add that contrary to Huttington, Islamic terrorists' attacks on western targets are not 'rooted in a deep and long-running civilizational conflict' but rather 'the consequence of the high strategic value of attacking Westerners' (Neumayer and Plumper, 2009, p 720). They put that 'western interference' in the country or region of Islamic terrorists provide 'additional incentives' for targeting western interests at reach (Neumayer and Plumper, 2009, p 720). For them, Huttington's clash of civilization is a 'cultural theory', ill-equipped to understand the patterns of international terrorism (Neumayer and Plumper, 2009, p 733).

II. On Local, Regional, Global Peacekeeping mechanisms in Post-cold war Africa

Post-colonial Africa has seen the rise of internal conflicts with regional effects since the end of the Cold War (Mateos and Grasa, 2009). However, the pattern chosen by countries of the region to guarantee their security vary from Francophone to Anglophones, from military strong to weak states. When its protracted crisis climaxed in 2012, Mali has chosen to involve France, its former colonial master, ECOWAS and AU, key regional actors within the APSA and the UNSC, main international body in charge of global security issues. The EU also launched EUTM-Mali to train Mali army while the US provided logistical assistance to France operation.

The multiplicity of actors involved with an overlapping mandate and equipped with different capabilities and upbringings ought to be addressed theoretically to detect the specificity and originality of the pattern chosen by Mali to address its crisis. Mali pattern is apprehended in the settings of post-colonial Africa defense and security mechanisms in the aftermath of the cold war era.

Contrary to other colonial powers, Great Britain for example, France has always sought actively to keep a tight sphere d'influence in its former colonies

(Adeniji, 1997). France 'cooperation agreements' were also part of the conditionalities for African countries seeking independence (Adeniji, 1997). Francophone Africa then became France's pré-carré, 'hostage' of its former colonizer through this 'special relationship' (Adeniji, 1997).

Patterns of cooperation between colonial powers and colonies in Africa focused essentially on 'policy of linking colonies with mechanisms of common services' whether economic, military or technological (Adeniji, 1997). 'For French West Africa, integration was deeper' and included attempt to federate territories, the development of a common currency and central Bank and more importantly, defense agreements (Adeniji, 1997).

This is part of the reasons 'France intervened militarily in Africa nineteen times between 1962 and 1995' (Hansen, 2008). Cited by Hansen, Shaun Gregory adds that France 'standard for military support was contingent on an African leader's willingness to support French interests' (Hansen, 2008). Controversial France military operations in Africa reached a decisive moment when French military intervened in Rwanda Genocide in 1994 and were accused of supporting and training Hutu genocidal government (Hansen, 2008).

Following Rwanda experience, France attempted to reshape its Africa military policy and sought to frame its future interventions in the context and structures of international peacekeeping arrangements and African regional bodies (Hansen, 2008). However, this multilateral façade seems to be designed further beyond the past failures of French interventionism and include dimensions of 'offsetting the political, military, diplomatic, and financial costs of formerly national operations' (Utley quoted by Hansen, 2008). This budgetary constraint is visible in sharp reduction of France military and 'base closures between 1997 and 2002' (Hansen, 2008).

In addition, successive French political leaders elaborated on the useless burden of Francafrique policies and claimed to be in rupture with those shortcomings (Hansen, 2008). In fact, nothing seems to have changed and a statement released in 2010 by France's exiting ambassador from Senegal, Jean-Christophe Rufin stated that 'African affairs' were run directly from the Presidential Palace and French diplomats in Africa were simply 'completely marginalized' (Crumley, 2010).

Moreover, recent developments, in particular Mali crisis have seen the re-engagement of France military in Africa and a reinforcement of France military presence in the continent (Melly and Darracq, 2013). It is suggested that Opération Serval bolstered France confidence to 'stage high-risk emergency intervention' in the continent and French government's White Paper on defense policy, published on 29 April 2013, explicitly recognizes 'a particular role for Africa' in national defence and security strategy (Melly and Darracq, 2013).

Post-colonial Africa vertical links with former colonial powers severed horizontal links of regional integration (Adeniji, 1997). Specifically there was a clear divide between Francophone and Anglophone in Western Africa which weakened initiatives of regional integration (Adeniji, 1997). This was evident when Ghana was accused by its Francophone neighbors of 'alleged subversive activities' which resulted in the 'Declaration on the Problem of Subversion' when Ghana hosted OAU summit in 1965 (Adeniji, 1997). Furthermore, first initiatives of regional integration in Western Africa were created along language and colonial past divisions. That is the case of West African Customs Union or West African Economic Community (CEAO) for Francophone West Africa. When broader initiatives of regional integration where initiated, the language barrier hampered its establishment since they were fears that Nigeria, a powerful Anglophone country could dominate the organizations (Adeniji, 1997). These are circumstances of 'first proposal by the Economic Commission for Africa (ECA) for the creation of an Economic Community of West African States' (Adeniji, 1997).

Additionally, first proposals for regional integration in West Africa were driven by economic agendas (Adeniji, 1997). ECOWAS, the first body to bring all western African countries did not even feature defense and security concerns in its preamble while the sub-region was already subjected to security threats (Adeniji, 1997). However, inter-state conflicts in the region prompted ECOWAS and CEAO to set out mechanisms and protocols into the field of peace and security (Adeniji, 1997). ECOWAS signed the protocol of Non-Aggression in 1978 and the protocol relating to Mutual Assistance on Defence 1981 and the CEAO put in place the ANAD mechanism in 1977 after border war between Burkina Faso and Mali (Adeniji, 1997).

ECOWAS and CEAO competitive instruments in the field of peace and security weakened both institutions, especially CEAO which was built around common language mantra in a multi-lingual sub-region by a set of military weak Francophone nations and could not survive on the long-term because of a 'waning of interest among the parties' in favour of wider ECOWAS scope (Adeniji, 1997).

At the continental level, OAU Mechanism for Conflict Prevention, Management and Resolution (OAU-MCPMR) was established in 1993, right after the progressive fading of the Cold War and thirty years after the organization was launched. Before this mechanism, it is argued that the OAU was successful in handling border disputes on the continent (Vogt and Muyangwa, 2000). Also, it is contented that the cold war provided 'an appreciable level of stability in Africa in the 1970s and 80s due principally to super power rivalry' which refrained OAU from playing a prominent role in conflict management in favor of the UN Security Council (Dike, 2010).

The end of the cold war witnessed the eruption of intra-states and the waning of inter-states conflicts in Africa (Dike, 2010). This new security situation was enabled by the fading of cold war rivalry and the lack of interest of the emerging order to deal with pressing security issues in the continent (Dike, 2010). Also, OAU, fashioned 'to contend with the challenges of cold war conflict dynamics' was ill-equipped to deal with the new threats of internal and transnational conflicts (Dike, 2010). OAU actions were limited by the provisions of its charter which prohibited intervention in member states 'internal affairs' (Vogt and Muyangwa, 2000).

Even if, the OAU-MCPMR was tailored at the end of cold war to deal with pressing internal threats, an assessment of the mechanism 7 years later proven that the OAU still lacked the capacity, resource and experience to defuse and resolve conflicts by itself (Vogt and Muyangwa, 2000).

This logically prompted the transmutation of the OAU into the AU which has been more ambitious in setting peace and security at its core and allowing the organization to intervene in its member states in grave circumstances. The AU robust constitutive act allowed it to put in place an elaborated continental peace and security architecture, the APSA, enshrined in the peace and security protocol.

APSA rests on five pillars and include the RECs as a key stalwart of the architecture. Authors agree that APSA has the potential to 'transform the way the continent addresses the mutually constituted challenges of peace, security and development' (Engel and Porto, 2010, p 143). However, they point out that this innovative approach comes with no ready-made templates or recipe and implies new risks to be taken to implement and actualize it (Engel and Porto, 2010, p 143).

Another area of research is the relationship of APSA with relevant UN mechanisms on peace and security namely the UNSC. The UNSC was endowed with the primordial mandate to address global security issues. Though, Jackie Cilliers reveals that a new paradigm is unfolding which consist of burden sharing between the UN and subregional bodies, in occurrence the AU and its APSA (Cilliers, 2010). In his sense, this trend is particularly vivid in Africa and must be 'unpacked' and exposed', 'given the limited potential of state-centred, region-based initiatives' (Cilliers, 2010).

After exploring key arguments and discussing previous researches in domains pertaining to the convolution of Mali crises in 2012 and 2013, it is logic to move and set the context to untangle the intersecting crises that troubled the country.

Chap III. Anatomy of the Context and Disentanglement of Mali Crises

The year 2012 saw Mali, a state once praised for its 'democratic' model, utmost collapse. Embroiled in a set of systemic inter-connected and complex self-reinforcing crises, the country had to rely on its bilateral, regional and global partners to avoid breakdown.

Before the situation was rotten enough for insurgency and state near collapse, Mali conflict evolved in a milieu set apart with an unprecedented concentration of tangled crises (Sow, 2013). Each of these crises triggers and drivers derived from specific logics not mutually exclusive but intertwined and sometimes nurturing each other (Sow, 2013).

An attempt to disentangle Mali crises system result into distinguishing between three distinct but interacting sub-crises namely: (1) Touareg nationalist/secessionist conflict engrained in longstanding resistance and grievances in a post-slavery and post-colonial context; (2) Transnational/Regional Djihadism creed conflict run by AQIM and its allies especially Ansar Dine and MUJAO, sustained by smuggling, ransoms and transnational organized crimes in a post-cold war setting; (3) Acute political and governance crisis embroiled in a greed-driven web of international assistance in a post-colonial African state challenged by Mbembe's 'belly' and 'phallus'.

Figure 2 - Dimensions and Conflict Dynamics in Mali (2012-2013)

III.1. Touareg Protracted Crisis: Nationalism and Secessionism

First of all, the illusion that Touaregs, a collection of tribes scattered in an area encompassing Mali, Niger, Algeria and Libya are bound by 'an organic primordial solidarity' is false (Marchal, 2012). Roland Marchal, in an attempt to move beyond the classic 'reification and oversimplification' exhibited in many international media, describe the Touaregs as a 'loose confederation of loose units' embroiled in internal differences in addition to political and social categories, between noble and plebeian, migrant and autochthone or youth and elder (Marchal, 1012, p 4). However, they quickly take side together when it comes to defend and promote their common identity.

This time, they endeavored to enact their own nation-state and contributed to trigger a regional crisis entrenched in 'the emergence of new regimes of territorisalisation' and space construct in the continent (Engel and Nugent, 2009, p 6). Scholars argue that these fresh dynamics are parcel of the massive 'respacing' occurring in Africa at the margin of classic nation-states of the continent (Engel and Nugent, 2009). Mali experience shows that these emerging and changing aspects of space creation while challenging the classic nation-state legitimacy might not be resilient enough to erode its territory in a sustainable way.

A salient observation on the country demography reveals that Touaregs accounts for less than ten percent of the country's population, yet their successive rebellions have durably affected the country in its postcolonial history (Thurston and Lebovitch, 2013).

Deep-rooted analysis reveals that Mali crisis first originates from old Touareg grievances engrained in secessionist-nationalist claims amid rampant rearmament following the downfall of Gaddaffi regime and increased revenues from smuggling and transnational organized crime. In what they call a 'divided north', Lecocq et al. position northern Mali conflict in the spectrum of 'rooted social distinctions' and 'racial difference' that they 'grossly oversimplified' in the notions of "white" Tuareg and Arabs, and "black African" Songhay and other communities' (2013, p 2).

41

These scholars pursue that post-colonial Mali is the fief of 'competing racial nationalisms' especially between Touaregs and Songhays (Lecocq et al., 2013, p 2). History seems to follow this analysis for the reason that shortly after Mali independence from France in 1960, Touareg launched their first rebellion movement in 1962 called Alfellaga. According to Baz Lecocq, Alfellaga rebellion is a 'genealogical continuity' of Touaregs resistance to external rule firstly against colonizers (Even if, he concedes that they collaborated with France but never fell under control of the colonial power) and then against the authorities and laws of newly independent Mali (2010). Citing a famous Touareg resistant, he states that in addition to refusing the authority of Mali, one of the main reason was that Touaregs 'nomads of the white race, can neither conceive nor accept to be commanded by blacks whom *[they]* always had as servants and slaves' (Lecocq, 2010, p 159). Lecocq in the logic of Gregory Mann sees Mali as a country were the post-colonial and post-slavery are intertwined namely in what he calls the 'bellah question' (Lecocq, 2010, p 76).

Mali brutally repressed Alfellaga rebellion but could not succeed to deepen the nationalist sentiment in Touaregs areas. Instead, the repression of Alfellega generated latent grievances and a need for revenge carried in the memories of Touareg 'genealogical continuity' (Lecocq, 2010, p 76). Alexander Thurston and Andrew Lebovich recounts the 1970's drought in northern Mali which dispersed Touaregs in Northern African Countries such as Libya and into refugee camps while the international assistance failed or disappeared in 'corrupt pockets of government officials' nurturing Touareg grievances and the forming of the Tanekra movement, 'a plan for "uprising" in Mali' with the 'political goal of an independent state in the Sahara, one that would encompass parts of Mali and Niger' (2013, p 22).

The ensued second Touareg rebellion lasted six years from 1990 to 1996 in the context of the end of cold war and transition to a multiparty system and 'democracy' in Mali. This rebellion was the corollary of Chad war in 1986 where Touaregs fighters defected from Libyan Army after it was crushed by Chadian and French troops and went back to Mali and Niger with their weapons (Keita, 1998). The second Touareg rebellion is distinguished by sporadic attacks and subsequent attempts by successive regimes in Bamako to settle peace deal. The first peace deal was the Accords of Tamanrasset signed on January 6, 1991 between Moussa Traore's regime and Touareg rebels under Algerian umbrella and launched a framework for Touareg integration in the Malian administration and army (Keita, 1998). Touaregs privileges during the integration period generated resentment in other communities particularly the Songhays who decided to rally into the Ganda Koy movement (Keita, 1998).

Keita analysis goes beyond Lecocq racial perspective. He points to hostilities between Ganda Koy and Touaregs stressing 'economic dimensions' of North Mali problems to 'communities […] fighting for scarce resources' (1998, p 20). Nevertheless, a peace settlement was finally negotiated in 1996 and the ceremony of the 'flame of peace' celebrating Malian unity culminated with the burning of more than 3000 weapons from rebel fighters in Timbuktu (Lecocq, 2010, p 6).

In 1998, Keita suggested that this second peace dealt decisively with 'the root causes as well as the symptoms of the conflict' (p 29). In his words, the flame of peace 'is a case in which democratic reform survived the challenge of ancient hatreds' (Keita, 1998, p 29). This argument was challenged a decade later by another Touareg rebellion with growing sporadic attacks from 2007 to 2009 in Northern Mali and Niger.

Moreover, in 2010, Baz Lecocq perceived that 'egha', a Touareg 'continuum of resistance' concept including 'a mixture of hate; powerlessness; and longing for

43

revenge' might be still alive for the reason that 'the atrocities committed during the first rebellion were repeated in the second rebellion' (2010, p 314).

The fourth Touareg rebellion which started in Northern Mali on January 2012 seems to follow 'egha' continuity of resistance pattern. However, the nationalist/secessionist Touareg rebellion appears henceforth embedded in transnational and regional Djihadism. The next apart will assess the specificity of the third rebellion precisely the interacting agendas within the Touareg secessionist and the political Islamists.

III.2. 2012-2013 Touareg and Islamist Terrorist Crisis: Colluding and Competing Agendas

The fourth Touareg rebellion has been analyzed as 'the most serious threat ever from the Tuaregs' bolstered by their new arsenal and their alliance with radical Islamists (Nossiter, 2012). Many suggests that the 2012 rebellion in Northen Mali is a spillover effect of NATO war in Libya and the overthrow of Gadhafi regime complicated by the war on terror in the Sahel (Nossiter, 2012; Lecocq et al., 2012; Mann, 2012). Other moves from the logistic and military facet of the insurgency and contends that 'neither Gaddafi's fall nor AQIM are the prime movers' adding that these are just 'fresh opportunities and circumstances in a very old struggle' of Touaregs for a nation-state of their own (Morgan, 2012).

Nevertheless, there is overall agreement that this rebellion is different from the previous pattern of cyclic 'failure' and ad-hoc attacks which set up the previous ones. Morgan for example submits that the 2012 rebellion was planned since 2009 by Ibrahim Ag Bahanga during his exile in Libya (2012). Morgan believes that this rebellion was better organized with an intellectual wing, the MNA at its debit in 2010 that he nicknames the 'Sahara's Facebook generation' (Morgan, 2012). According to him, the MNLA has achieved 'a better balanced and multi-faceted movement' with the inclusion of the 'internet generation' rebels in the movement to solve the 'eternal problem of disunity' among Touregs' (Morgan, 2012). Roland Marchal argues that 'this civilian component of the MNLA' was inspired by the 'Arab spring' and was seeking a referendum of self-determination like in South-Sudan (2012, p 7).

Movement Acronym	Ideology	Aims	Date of Creation	Main Leader(2012)
MNLA	☞ Secularist (But deeply enmeshed with Mali Islamic Culture)	☞ Secessionism ☞ Creation of AZAWAD	☞ 2011	☞ Bilal Ag Chérif (Secretary-General of the MNLA)
MAA	☞ Secular Arab nationalism	☞ Secessionism ☞ Creation of AZAWAD	☞ 2012 (Split from MNLA)	☞ Ahmed Ould Sidi Mohamed
Ansar-Dine	☞ Political Islamism	☞ Creation of an Islamic State in Mali	☞ 2012	☞ Iyad Ag Ghaly
AQIM	☞ Radical Islamism, Jihadism, Salafism	☞ Creation of an Islamic caliphate in Algeria and the Maghreb region	☞ 2007	☞ Mokhtar Belmokhtar (The One-Eyed)
MUJAO	☞ Radical Islamism, Jihadism, Salafism	☞ Creation of an Islamic caliphate in Western Africa	☞ 2011 (Split from AQIM)	☞ Hamada Ould Mohamed Kheirou (Abu Qumqum)

Figure 3 - Matrix of main rebel movements in Mali (2012-2013), their ideology, aims and leaders

III.2.1. Circumstantial Alliance of MNLA Secessionism and Radical Islamism: Effect of Colluding Agendas

Interesting enough is that from its onset in 2011, the MNLA argued in favor of a secular society and the rejection of radical Islamism as its ideology. This is visible with the sidelining of Iyad Ag Ghali candidacy to the post of Secretary General of the MNLA (Morgan, 2012). Ghali has appeared as a prominent figure of radical Islam in Mali since his conversion by Pakistani missionaries in the late 1990s according to Gregory Mann (2012). Put aside and ostracized in the MNLA, Iyad Ag Ghali splitted from it and founded Ansar Dine ("defenders of the faith" in Arabic) late 2011, a Salafi movement aimed at instituting sharia as the ruling law in AZAWAD and beyond in the whole Mali (Morgan, 2012).

Moreover, Ansar Dine is not the only radical Islamist movement active in the region. AQIM is seen by many as the oldest Islamist and terrorist organization operating in Sahel and originating from the failure of GIA and GSPC during Algerian civil war from 1992 to 2000 (Thurston and Lebovitch, 2013). To avert Algerian retaliation and to capture tourists in order to sustain its economic survival, GSPC moved southward into the ungoverned spaces of Malian Sahel to later merged with Al Qaida in 2006-2007 and rename itself AQMI (Thurston and Lebovitch, 2013).

Jessica Huckabey argues that analyses revealed that AQIM also suffered internal dissensions caused by the divergence of view over the leadership and scope of the terrorist organization (2013). They were complaint that Algerian dominated AQIM and that its terrorist activities were mostly directed towards Algiers regime (Huckabey, 2013). These dissensions led to the creation of MUJAO, Movement for Unicity and Jihad in West Africa led by Hamada Ould Mohammed Kheirou in October 2011 with the purpose to "impose sharia across the whole of west Africa" and target France (Huckabey, 2013). Therefore, the terrorist movement main target is the regional western African spaces and beyond it seeks to be involved into the global 'war on terror' (Huckabey, 2013).

According to Roland Marchal, MUJAO did not split from AQIM, but was rather born from it (2012, p 10). For him, this is a tactic of delegation used by AQIM in order to muster local ground for the movement in the region based on al-Qaeda principle of 'centralization of decision-making and decentralization of execution' (Marchal, 2012, p 10).

An interesting dimension in the presence of various radical Islamist movements in Northern Mali embedded in the vast open and desert spaces of Sahel is the hasty analogy with Afghanistan or Somalia as seen by Zyck and Muggah (2013, p 3). The concept of 'Africanistan' with regards to the 'Afghanisation' or 'Somalisation' of Mali is broke down as 'inaccurate and unhelpful' (Salah cited by Zyck and Muggah, 2013, p 3). Moreover, Gregory Mann evaluates that some African diplomats have played the 'Africanistan' card in Mali in order to hasten international intervention but decisively contends that while there might be similarities, Mali 'is not exactly' Afghanistan and must be approached as such (Mann, 2012).

Another facet of the rebellion was the activity of Al-Qaeda Global Islamist network with reported presence in masse of Boko Haram Salafi fighters from Nigeria who arrived to support MUJAO and other Al Qaeda-affiliated movements like Ansar al-Charia from Libya who came to reinforce their ideological comrades during this decisive endeavor (Huckabey, 2013; John Irish and Bate Felix, 2013). Thus, there is a plethora of movement involved in Mali conflict ranging from nationalist/secessionist to radical Islamist and global terrorist movements.

Hence, these movements might diverge in their ideologies and overall ambitions or strategies. However, they share a convergent interest which is to enlarge controlled spaces and territories. Thus, despite their differences, leaders of MNLA, Ansar Dine, AQIM and MUJAO met on December 7, 2011 in order to plan an 'imminent offensive' in Malian territory (Alvarado, 2012). This alliance has been described as an 'Alliance of Circumstances' where these movements made a strategic benefit from the domestic void and regional settings in Norther Mali at the end of 2011 (Alvarado, 2012).

Consequently, this coalition of heavily armed movements launched its first attacks on 17 January 2012 successively in Menaka, Tessalit and Aguelhoc where they slaughtered, using an Al-Qaeda technique, more than hundred Malian troops in what was labelled 'Aguelhoc massacre' (Théroux-Bénoni et Al., 2012). ISS scholars points out that Aguelhoc massacre was facilitated by the 'duplicity' of certain officers, most problably the so-called Touaregs 'intégrés' who were hired in the army to cool down previous insurgency and quickly defected to join MNLA and its allies when the rebellion re-started (Théroux-Bénoni et Al., 2012, p 3). They also criticize the meagre logistic of Malian army in comparison to the rebel arsenal as well as the maladministration of the army in the north and its negligence by Bamako army (Théroux-Bénoni et Al., 2012).

Aguelhoc massacre was a terrible choc for the country and triggered manifestations in Bamako with the wives of slaughtered soldiers claiming that their husbands were simply sent to be exterminated without any governmental support (Anne Doquet cited by Marie de Douhet, 2012). The operational mode also confirmed the presence of Al-Qaeda affiliated movements within the rebellion and prompted regional and international harsh reactions namely from the ECOWAS and the AU and key powers such as US and France. Moreover, the International Criminal Court prosecutor later in January 2013 opened a case to investigate this blatant violation of Geneva conventions and war crime under the terms of the ICC Statute.

Boisbouvier has reported the MNLA spokesperson asserting that MNLA did not commit any massacre or killing anyone in Aguelhoc and recounted that a gap exists between his movement and AQIM-affiliated movements (2012). For others, there was confusion around the relation between the MNLA and the Islamists from the onset obvious in their confusing communication strategy (Lecocq et al., 2013, p 7). They suggest that 'Ansar Dine leader [...] counted on the MNLA's media capacities' and doubt the military capabilities of the MNLA (Lecocq et al., 2013, p 7). Further, they construe the MNLA as a weedy organization relying on the victory of its Islamist allies and taking credit for the victories while trying to distance itself from their operational mode and ideologies (Lecocq et al., 2013). They also submit that economically and military stronger Islamists of Ansar Dine and MUJAO were able to attract 'a core of experienced MNLA fighters from the Kidal Region' weakening its military likewise (Lecocq et al., 2013, p 8).

Lacking basic ammunitions and feeling completely abandoned by the military command chain, the Malian army did not offer much of a resistance (Mann, 2012). This is confirmed by the declarations of Lt. Col. Diarran Kone of Malian Defense Ministry who admitted to the New York Times that rebels' weaponry was 'significant enough to allow them to achieve their objectives' (Nossiter, 2012). ISS Researchers also points out that the Malian army was neither equipped nor trained to fight such insurgency given the opacity of its recruitment system (Theroux-Benoni et al., 2012). This will be investigated in details in the next part but it is evident that there is a connection between the botched governance in Bamako and the stampede of the army in the North.

On the other hand, the unraveling rebellion alliance profited from this power vacuum to swiftly invade other cities in the region. They reportedly took the key town of Tessalit on 11 March 2012 including its military base after fierce battle involving US logistic assistance to Mali army[24]. They also conquered the strategic town of Tinzawaten at Mali-Algeria border, a vital transit space for smuggling and other transnational organized criminal activities occurring in the Saharan desert[25].

Confident on its swift successes, the rebellion boycotted the invitation to Algiers for talks about a cease fire agreement. For MNLA representatives, the cease fire call in Algiers is useless and the only solution for them is to organize negotiations on self-determination for AZAWAD in a neutral country involving UN delegates[26]. Conversely, manifestations in Bamako intensified and a mutiny started short after the Defense Minister went to address the Army in its garrison town of Kati on 21 March 2012. The young mutineers toppled Amani Toumani Touré (ATT) regime the next day and created the CNRDE (National Committee for the Re-establishment of Democracy and the Restoration of the State) justified by the incapacity of ATT regime to provide necessary logistics for the army to defend Malian territory (Mann, 2012).

These circumstances and the chaotic situation following the junta appeared as atouitas ("godsend" in Tamasheq, Touareg dialect) tragedies that prompted the rebellion to speedily move southward. So they started to put a considerable

---

[24] See RFI (International France Radio) article 'La ville de Tessalit, au nord du Mali, est aux mains des rebelles du MNLA' at http://www.rfi.fr/afrique/20120312-nord-mali-ville-tessalit-rebelles-mnla-touaregs/ and the StrategyPage article 'Logistics: American Robots Sustain The Siege of Tessalit' at http://www.strategypage.com/htmw/htlog/articles/20120308.aspx, accessed April 2014.
[25] See Reuters article 'Malian rebels seize key border town, civilians flee' at http://af.reuters.com/article/maliNews/idAFL5E8D8A0G20120209, accessed May 2014.
[26] See AFP (Agence France Presse) article 'Tuareg rebels not bound by truce talks' at http://www.news24.com/Africa/News/Tuareg-rebels-not-bound-by-truce-talks-20120207 and Afrik.com article 'Mali: le MNLA refuse l'appel au cessez-le-feu proposé par Alger' at http://www.afrik.com/breve38947.html, accessed May 2014.

pressure on Kidal, a regional capital of the region that they finally captured on 30 March 2012 without much resistance from the junta[27]. After Kidal, they took Gao another regional capital the next day, 31 March 2012 and then Timbuktu, the following day, latest regional capital to fall into the hands of the MNLA and its Islamist terrorist circumstantial allies[28].

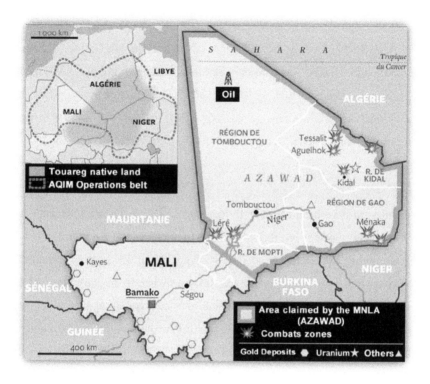

Figure 4 - A map showing the territory of AZAWAD claimed by the MNLA as well as the main combats areas and mineral deposits in Mali

---

[27] See RFI article 'La ville de Kidal, dans le nord du Mali, prise par les rebelles' at http://www.rfi.fr/afrique/20120330-ville-kidal-le-nord-mali-prise-rebelles/, accessed May 2014.

[28] See BBC article 'Mali Tuareg rebels control Timbuktu as troops flee' at http://www.bbc.com/news/world-africa-17576725 and MALIWEB article 'Mali: les rebelles prennent Tombouctou, le Mali coupé en deux' at http://www.maliweb.net/la-situation-politique-et-securitaire-au-nord/le-mali-coupe-en-deux-57997.html, accessed May 2014.

So, on 01 April 2012, MNLA and Islamists controlled all the regional capitals of the claimed AZAWAD that they sought to administer. After the capture of the desired portion of territory, the MNLA declared unilaterally and 'irrevocably the Independent State of AZAWAD' on 06 April 2012[29]. The declaration was published on its website and was unanimously rejected by the African Union and the United Nations as well as all key regional and global powers (Liu, 2012). In an article entitled 'The Rise of Wikipedian Statecraft: How Azawad, Spurned by the U.N., Earned Its Recognition Online', Jonathan Liu derided MNLA declaration of independence and its Wikipedia independence attempt, stating that even if no foreign government or international organization recognized AZAWAD, its leaders succeeded at least to secure 'the most critical "recognition" of all' using Wikipedia (2012).

In addition to have been consistently denied its self-proclaimed independence, MNLA leaders also have to face growing dissentions within the coalition which was crumbling days after days. For example, Ansar Dine openly contested MNLA wish to form a secular AZAWAD state when its military chief, Omar Hamaha said 'it's a legal war in the name of Islam. We are against rebellions. We are against independence. We are against revolutions not in the name of Islam'[30]. Clearly, Ansar Dine emir, Iyad Ag Ghali detailed during a public meeting that his objective was not AZAWAD but Islam (Diop, 2012). Iyad

---

[29] See MNLA 'Déclaration d'indépendance de l'AZAWAD' at
http://www.mnlamov.net/index.php?view=article&id=169:declaration-dindependance-de-lazawad&tmpl=component&print=1&layout=default&page=, accessed May 2014.
[30] See AFP article 'Global powers dismiss Tuaregs' declared independence' at
http://www.france24.com/en/20120406-world-rejects-tuareg-independence-declaration-north-mali-rebel-international-community-azawad/, accessed May 2014.

added that Mali was enough as a state and that Ansar Dine aimed to spread its version of Islam within that space (Diop, 2012)[31].

Notwithstanding Ansar Dine clear call to sharia, MNLA still sought to formalize its alliance with the movement in order to erect AZAWAD national army (Mahjar-Barducci, 2012). Despite the signature of a Memorandum of Understanding between both movements on 26 May 2012, no agreement was reached since the MNLA feared to be connected with Ansar Dine terrorist membership and sidelined definitively by external powers (Mahjar-Barducci, 2012).

Then again, AQIM and its upshots did not care much about MNLA dream of AZAWAD and started to apply their peculiar sharia law within the local communities. They were accused by Human Rights Watch of inflicting violent 'huddud' punishments as well as harassing people suspected of forbidden 'haram' activities[32]. These reports adding to the dramatic imposition of 'modesty and veiling' to women 'made for extraordinarily bad press abroad [...] combined with direct threats against neighboring states' (Lecocq et al., 2012).

III.2.2. Ending of an Unnatural Alliance: Competing Agendas amid MNLA Secessionism and Radical Islamism

Irreconcilable disputes about ideology as well as the ultimate aim of the rebellion triggered an epic battle among the former 'circumstantial' allies involving the nationalist of the MNLA against an alliance of the controversial

---

[31] See Mame Diarra DIOP article 'Tombouctou sous la menace de la Charia' at
http://www.journaldumali.com/article.php?aid=4447, accessed May 2014.
[32] See Human Rights report 'Mali: Islamist Armed Groups Spread Fear in North' at
http://www.hrw.org/news/2012/09/25/mali-islamist-armed-groups-spread-fear-north, accessed May 2014.

Islamist terrorists including Ansar Dine, AQMI and MUJAO. In the space of few weeks, MNLA nationalists were rooted out of the claimed homeland of AZAWAD by a military stronger alliance of Islamists and terrorists of Ansar Dine, AQIM and MUJAO (Lecocq et al., 2012). On June 27, Iyad and his terrorist fellows had managed to dislodge MNLA secessionists from their stronghold in GAO and started bossing northern Mali.

Interestingly, AQIM and its associates sought to craft some sort of legitimacy especially among the young population. In an attempt to 'win hearts and minds', they were seen 'doling out cash and other gifts' (Palus, 2012). In addition, many recounts that AQIM did not refrain from enrolling, sometimes coercively, children and youths driven by economic survival without any other perspective at the time (Palus, 2012; Lecocq et al., 2012). Nancy Palus argues that AQIM benevolences originated from stolen and confiscated humanitarian aid entering the area (2012). For her, the balance of this complex mix of punishment and charity quickly degenerated and there were growing uproar among the locals who protested actively against what was perceived as an alien crusade in that part of Mali (Palus, 2012).

Therefore, protests rose among locals of the region against the strange sharia rule of AQIM and its subsidiaries. The revolt quickly spread to the city of Kidal on 06 June 2012, led by women and youths seeking to defy Ansar Dine who 'repressed these demonstrations with beatings, whippings or by firing in the air' (Lecocq et al., 2012). Grippingly, women led the resistance from Kidal as well as from Paris where Aïchata Haïdara, a congresswoman native of Timbuktu sounded the alarm about the degradation of the situation of youths and women under the rule of Islamists and the MNLA (Védrines, 2012). For Nina Wallet Intalou, a charismatic Touareg woman affiliated to the MNLA and exiled in

Mauritania, AQIM was simply fighting their culture embodied in MNLA nationalist aspirations (Mandraud, 2012)[33].

Conceivably, the paramount mistake made by Ansar Dine Islamists happened on 30 June 2012 in the renowned town of Timbuktu, baptized the city of 333 Islam saints, where they undertook the destruction of 15th century ancient mausoleums covering Sufi Islam saints shrines seen by the group as 'idolatrous' but registered in UNESCO world heritage database in 1988 (Lister, 2013; Callimachi, 2013). Sheer bad timing or strategy (or a combination of all the above), these monuments were added few days ago on 28 June 2012, on the list of UNESCO endangered world heritage at the request of interim Malian authorities (Lister, 2013; Callimachi, 2013). Plausibly, a communication tactic from Ansar Dine, it opened the eyes of global powers to the budding risks of Mali crisis and alienated utterly the Islamists local support (Callimachi, 2013).

At the local level, people of Timbuktu felt that their city was 'raped'[34] and concluded that the game was over with the brutal Islamists (Callimachi, 2013). Many local Sufi Muslims reasoned that Ansar Dine and MUJAO Islamists could not claim to teach Islam to Malians which had established since centuries 'well-developed Islamic intellectual culture' (Lecocq et al., 2012, p 13). Furthermore, Ansar Dine emir, Iyad Ag Ghali had completely wasted his remaining support among fellow Touaregs tribesmen following the ruthlessness of his troops among the population and his persistence to collaborate with AQIM in spite of the demand of traditional authorities' to refrain to do so (Lecocq et al., 2012, p 12).Scholars believe that Iyad, an experimented player in

---

[33] See Le Monde article 'Nina Wallet Intalou, la pasionaria indépendantiste des Touareg maliens' written by Isabelle Mandraud, accessed May 2014.

[34] A source close to a local imam cited by Al Arabiya News reportedly said "They have raped Timbuktu today. It is a crime" at http://english.alarabiya.net/articles/2012/06/30/223630.html, accessed May 2014.

Malian political arena, played an equivocal game shaped to keep 'Ansar Dine as the sole viable alternative' in the rebellion (Lecocq et al., 2012, p 12).

When it became clear that external intervention was imminent, Iyad overlooked his project of Islamic caliphate in Mali and Ansar Dine apparently desisted to cooperate with AQIM and MUJAO[35]. This dramatic shift in Ansar Dine raison d'être at the same time in creed and stratagem was surely motivated by Iyad rationale that the rebellions were to be crushed by the upcoming international interventions and his wish to appear as a credible interlocutor available to help fix complex skirmishes of Northern Mali.

Fascinatingly, a confidential letter destined to AQIM-upshots in Mali, authenticated by renowned Islamologists and signed by AQIM emir, Abdel Malek Droukdel was found in Timbuktu after rebels fled the city to escape France intervention (Callimachi, 2013). In the document, Droukdel contested the approach of AQIM-affiliated movements in Northern Mali arguing that they needed to soften their slants and surprisingly, 'to slow down in implementing Shariah' because the Malian population was a small 'baby' that Islamists needed to fed step by step with their doctrine (Callimachi, 2013). The document revealed internal discord within AQMI over the strategy to rule Northern Mali and expose AQIM leadership in another light, beyond the classic terror rhetoric, a 'clear-headed, point-by-point' managed nebula (Callimachi, 2013). Some scholars also pointed to the racism existing in the group which tended to create a hierarchy between its members as well as between the local people based on skin color and shade and grounded in the regional society interactions (Huckabey, 2013; Lecocq et al; 2012).

---

[35] See Jeune Afrique article 'Crise malienne : Ansar Eddine change son fusil d'épaule' at http://www.jeuneafrique.com/Article/ARTJAWEB20121115084309/onu-mali-aqmi-cedeao-mali-crise-malienne-ansar-eddine-change-son-fusil-d-epaule.html, accessed May 2014.

2012-2013 rebellion finally proved to be the most complex and successful since Mali independence. Entrenched in an overarching mix of grievances, driven by creed and sustained by greed, it reminds of Frances Stewart model of Horizontal Inequalities discussed earlier, in the literature review.

Irrefutably, a web of ruthless, egotistical as well as ethno-centric deeds denied AQIM Islamists, the local legitimacy vital to unfold its regional 'Africanistan' agenda and deprived MNLA secessionists, the reverie of AZAWAD nation-state. Yet, Malian state institutions were not in better shape.

III.3. 2012-2013 Political and Constitutional crisis: Donor-driven Democracy and Power Vacuum

Mali political landscape sank into an abysmal confusion during years 2012 and 2013. From a praised democracy, the state collapsed into a junta and then convulsed during a transitional period undermined by factional battles over the remains of the state. It finally re-emerged as a facade of democracy after July 2013 elections. This section first assesses the limits of the Malian democracy and its governance system enmeshed in international donor strategic complacency and then moves to investigate the coup d'état of March 2012 and the tenuous and flickering ensuing transitional period. It also explores the power-play interactions within the transitional government ecosystem and its attitude in face of the growing pressure for international intervention.

III.3.1. ATT-cratie, Donor-Driven Democracy in a Post-colonial African State: Stretching 'belly' and 'phallus' to edges

There are many accounts on how Mali was described as a model democracy in Africa (Traub, 2012; Lewis, 2012; Lecocq et al., 2012; Whitehouse, 2012;

Marchal, 2012; Thurston, 2013). 2012 events in the country have proven that democracy does not equal to peace and stability as promoted by the democratic peace theory and its proponents.

Before the coup on 22 March 2012, ATT regime has accumulated flaws and was gradually undermined by a weak and ad-hoc governance model. As Robert D. Kaplan pointed out, a key challenge of African governments is to 'extend good governance and development far beyond the capitals' (2012).

Mali is a point in case. When ATT took over the country's presidency, he was widely acclaimed as the soldier of democracy. However, at the zenith of his rule, the country did not put much effort to extend its reach to the populations in the Northern area, therefore leaving massive 'ungoverned spaces' at the disposal of smugglers and terrorists who later worsened the contestation of its existence as nation-state throughout MNLA rebellion. Even in the capital, there was a growing feeling that the authorities were absent, like if Mali strongmen have vanished or simply resigned abandoning the country in a chaotic situation. Bruce Whitehouse (2012) suggests that people knew that power was henceforward in the 'street'.

ATT regime seemed more preoccupied to satisfy its 'belly' and 'phallus'. Mali follows Achille Mbembe postcolonial pattern of that African state where political elites are comparable to goat grazing wherever they are tied up (Mbembe, 1992, p7). In fact, research points that under ATT, the elites were much inclined to clientelism, corruption and nepotism (Lecocq et al., 2012; Marchal, 2012; Whitehouse, 2012). While Roland Marchal (2012) argues that increasing corruption had radically incapacitated and damped the country's army, Bruce Whitehouse (2012) suggests that beyond the clichés of democracy, there was obvious 'erosion of the rule of law' visible in the constant scorns inflicted by elected officials to the law to subserve their political interests and affiliations.

Before its downfall, ATT regime 'politique du ventre' did not even bother to hide its extravagance. Thus, Eros Sana (2013) recounts how ATT daughter pompously celebrate her multiple billions of Fcfa in Bamako in a sumptuous and grandiose party while soldiers where simply zombies abandoned by the hierarchy and unable to feed themselves. According to Le Sphinx (2007), ATT system installed impunity as a mode of governance driven by a 'nest of sharks'. That is the reason Malian democracy under ATT was labelled years earlier 'ATT-cratie' or a rule of a man and its clan (Le Sphinx, 2007). In addition, the malaise was exacerbated in the army by the old divisions between the red helmets favored by ATT and the green helmets treated as the subaltern others in the military (Sana, 2013). The army thus seemed to be caught in a zero-sum game between the green and red helmets, the rival corps constituting a vital share of its configuration.

Nevertheless, ATT policies where described as 'consensual' (Bergamaschi, 2008 and 2013; De Jorio, 2012; Wing, 2013; Robert and Heuer, 2007). For Rosa De Jorio (2012), ATT motivation was that 'African societies— characterized by social networks based on kinship and ethnic and regional affiliations—would disintegrate if they adopted the confrontational and argumentative logic of Western societies'.

However, according to Bergamaschi, ATT 'consensus-driven political system' castrated the opposition with the fear of marginalization from the national cake and also 'increasingly politicized the civil service while diminishing its performance' (2008, p 5-6). This is a clear indicator of a regime that did not strategize beyond its 'belly' and 'phallus'. So, it was logic that this regime of 'sharks' functioned similarly to a democracy of façade where 'supporters and opponents of Toumani Touré [confronted] each other in clearly outlined groups' (Robert and Heuer, 2007). The big picture and the experience from ATT democracy of façade is that 'All That Glitters Is Not Gold' (Robert and Heuer, 2007). According to RFI, ATT consensual politics were completely void of any substance in the last moments of power tenure since it had completely locked the political debate in Malian Medias[36].

Indeed, Ousmane Sow, a Malian journalist based in Canada perceived in 2008 that ATT was progressively 'washing his hands' off the presidential prerogatives of being the leader of Mali. For him, ATT linguistic blunder on 08 March 2008 when he was answering women's concerns about the growing challenges facing the country was whitewashed by the media in an unprecedented linguistics acrobatics (Sow, 2008). He reportedly said 'Bè b'i ba bolo' which simply means in Bambara 'do what you want' because the state can't help since it is impotent and toothless (Sow, 2008).

In addition to its self-seekingness, ATT regime was accused to be involved in smuggling and transnational organized crime. For example, Bergamaschi (2013) suggests that his government handed 'over thousands of acres of fertile land near the Office du Niger […] to international firms' and his clan was suspected to be in connection with the crash of a 'Boeing 727 - carrying six tonnes of cocaine from Latin America ' near Gao, in 2009. For her, Mali under ATT fits well in the polemical theory of 'criminal states' enacted by Bayart, Ellis and Hibou which investigates African governments' activities especially their propensity to be involved in illegal economic activities under the constraint of a web of exogenous factors Bergamaschi (2013) .

---

[36] See RFI article 'La chute d'Amadou Toumani Touré au Mali ou la défaite d'une politique de consensus' at http://www.rfi.fr/afrique/20120323-chute-amadou-toumani-toure-mali-defaite-une-politique-consensus/, accessed May 2014.

However, often, it is suggested that ATT regime attempted to stabilize and reassert its presence in the north by launching a flagship project, the Special Program for Peace, Security and Development in Northern Mali (PSPSDN) (Thiam, 2011; Daou, 2011; Wilandh, 2012). The rationale for PSPDN was that security problems in Northern Mali will be addressed by a strategy to re-occupy the space using a savant mix of increased military presence and local developmental initiatives (Thiam, 2011; Daou, 2011). Some thinks that PSPDN was specifically designed to address the flaws of 2006 agreement concluded in Algeria between the government and Touaregs rebels which completely demilitarized Northern Mali and created the authority void that AQIM and its allies later occupied (Wilandh, 2012).

The PSPSDN quickly unraveled and instead of sustaining its dualistic approach of a savant dosage indicated between increased military presence and local development, it focused almost exclusively on the military security aspect (Wilandh, 2012). For Malians, PSPSDN failed to engage the communities in the north and Susanna D. Wing (2013) adds that it reinforced 'the distance between the people and the government through the top-down process by which it was designed and implemented'. This open distance between the state and its population supplemented the web of factors that resuscitated Touareg rebellion of MNLA in 2012.

The failure of PSPSDN concurs to a thought-provoking and sometimes ignored angle to seize Mali downfall under ATT which is the tight intertwinement between Mali government and donor policies at the time. For Isaline Bergamaschi (2013 and 2008), Mali is a 'donor darling' entrenched in an intricate system of dependency towards its international patrons in a complex that she labels 'donor-driven ownership' meaning that 'there are few signs of genuine policy ownership and that the government lacks both the 'capacity' and 'political will' to pursue development goals and take the lead in the aid

61

relationship'. This opens a power vacuum which is progressively filled by the donors which henceforth drive the country's economic policies.

Bruce Whitehouse (2012) adds that in these circumstances, the government simply retires from crafting its own policies 'finding it simpler to accept donors' agendas'. He further analyses that this relation of dependency towards the donors disconnect the government from accountability mechanisms and widen the gap between it and the population it is supposed to serve (Whitehouse, 2012).

For example, Bergamaschi (2013) points to a new family code elaborated by donors aimed at 'modernizing Mali's Family Code' and voted by Mali parliament on July 3, 2009 which triggered harsh reactions in the Malian society especially among Islamic religious actors who seen it as the West interference or an 'external imposition and an attack on Malian tradition, religion and way of life'. The president finally backpedaled after a gigantic manifestation led by popular Imam in Bamako. This helped to consolidate Imams authority in a society who was caught in the rise of Islamism according to Gilles Holder (2011).

For Bergamaschi (2013), Mali dependency emanates from its historical trajectory of 'extraverted development' built from imported policies and the imposition of an alien state in accordance with Jean-Francois Bayard model of the African extraverted state. This argument is supplemented by Dambisa Moyo views that International aid is not working in Africa because it is trapped in a vicious cycle plagued by inefficient mechanisms of accountability which ease corruptions of elected officials and flaws the receiver economic development on the long term (2009).

This hybrid set of shortcomings led ATT regime to collapse when a simple mutiny turned into a coup d'état on 22 March 2012. For Gregory Mann (2012), the coup completely messed the political landscape of a country which was already suffocating from deeply enmeshed crises. The junta leader, Amadou Haya Sanogo blamed the coup on ATT regime inability to equip the army in order to deal with tense situation in the north (Bergamaschi, 2013).

III.2.1. Struggle over the Remnants of Mali: Power Vacuum during the Transition

Then again, the junta created the 'National Committee for the Re-establishment of Democracy and the Restoration of the State' (CNRDRE) in attempt to secure a space in the political arena. However, the unanimous condemnation the coup by regional powers as well as key international players added to the suspension of donor's flows and ECOWAS embargo pushed Sanogo and his fellows to relinquish the power to a transitional government formed two days after the putsch under the auspices of ECOWAS (Mann, 2012). Still, the junta leader sought to play a prominent role in the transition and contributed to the confusion and power struggle during the transitional government.

The transition period started on 24 March 2012 and aimed to put back the country on its feet by negotiating a peace agreement with MNLA and other moderate groups, setting the conditions for international interventions in order to dislodge AQIM from its stronghold in the north and organize the presidential elections in July 2013. Yet, the power-play and the fierce battle for political positioning within its officials threatened to worsen the country wounds.

The junta and the CNRDRE seemed to enjoy enough popularity especially in Bamako were they managed to secure the support of the notorious Omar

Mariko, a key figure of the anti-ATT and specifically, the junta secured the backing of the Coordination of Patriotic Organizations of Mali (COPAM), a radical movement who was openly opposed to the intervention of ECOWAS or France in the country (Coulibaly, 2012). It can emanate from the fear of Sanogo and his proponents to be sidelined and lost their upper-hand on the transition after an international intervention. The most interesting is that, COPAM which claims is to be a pan-Africanist movement was openly protesting against the involvement of a pan-African body to help redress Mali. An ICG reports add that COPAM leaders were young and denied any perspective during ATT regime and completely opposed to the 'old Malian elites' and 'foreign actors'[37].

Also, Cheick Modibo Diarra, a successful scientist with eminent careers in NASA and Microsoft was 'imposed' by ECOWAS with the backing of Sanogo as the Prime Minister of the transitional government (Lecocq et al., 2012, p 6). He was perceived by Malians as the worthy son of Soundjata[38] considering his lineage or the 'rare rich man' who 'earned his money honestly' outside of Mali Treasury (Lecocq et al., 2012, p 6). He was also given credit by scholars based on his prominent career. For example, Gregory Mann praised him as a 'possibility' to manage the 'mess in Mali' (2012). However, it was quickly clear that Diarra was 'politically tone deaf' and 'arrogant' to the extent that he alienated all the support that he enjoyed once from local elites not counting that of ECOWAS and key western capitals (Lecocq et al., 2012, Marchal, 2012). Roland Marchal adds that Diarra was referred as someone with an 'obtuse mind' driven by a blind thirst for power since he tried to appear as a 'technocrat' but had already created his own political party in March 2011 (Marchal, 2012). For him, Cheick Modibo Diarra was no more than the 'main Achilles' heel' of the transitional government.

---

[37] See ICG Africa Report N°189 of 18 July 2012 'MALI: AVOIDING ESCALATION'.
[38] Soundjata Keita was the King of Kings (Mansa) of the prosperous Kingdom of Mali in ancient times.

The transition government was headed by Professor Dioncounda Traore by virtue of his office as the head of the legislative body after ATT formally resigned. Traore was criticized for his tricks to stay in power after the transition and Roland Marchal claims that 'his enthusiasm was limited and his energy focused on the extension of his interim mandate' (2012, p 5). He was assaulted in his office on 21 May 2012 by a mob loyal to the junta and transferred to Paris for medical care letting Mali in a blatant power vacuum in the midst of its crisis. At his return in July, he appointed a new government that many observers analyzed as a simple continuity of the precedent quagmire with new faces (Lecocq et al., 2012, Marchal, 2012).

This fierce political battle by military and civilians on the remnants of the Malian state is the manifestation of a postcolonial Mali deep-seated in the 'grotesque' and 'obscene' and clearly demonstrate that the political elites battle in the post-ATT was not to help save the country, rather it was the continuity of the 'politique du ventre'.

ECOWAS and the international community actions were utterly annihilated by the power vacuum and the vanishing of a clearly articulated and legitimate Mali leadership during the tenuous transitional period. Efforts ongoing since the post-coup period took more than a year to produce palpable fruits and culminated in the signing of Ouagadougou agreement on 18 June 2013 paving the way to the organization of presidential elections in July 2013. The acclaimed election of Ibrahim Boubakar Keita, the new face of Mali 'democratie de facade' whitewashed by the community of donors and the hasty re-opening of the aid mammoth valves might trigger the return of old habits and jeopardize the efforts to shape a sustainable peace deal between the different cleavages founding the Malian nation.

Chap IV. Patterns of Conflict Resolution and Pitfalls

This part intends to assess the involvement of external actors, whether regional, continental or global key players in the process of conflict resolution of Mali crises during the years 2012 and 2013.

The direct partaking of France, ECOWAS, AU, UN is appraised, particularly the dynamics and the strategy of each of these actors given its specific relation with Mali, in the context of 'burden sharing' in peacekeeping arising as the norm between the UN and regional bodies. Also, the role of other key players as Algeria, US or the EU is given due consideration.

IV.1. 2012-2013 France Involvements in Mali Crisis: Before and During Operation Serval

France was the colonial power in Mali before the country gained its independence in 1960. France involvements in its former colonies or anywhere in Africa are often subject to controversy about the country's motivation and its alleged tight grip on its former colonies. During the 2012-2013 crises in Mali, France intervention unfolded first at diplomatic levels during 2012 and later at military level in 2013 with the launch of the operation codenamed Serval from an agile African cat.

The book assesses France contribution to settle Mali crisis by dissecting its overall strategy from the initial diplomatic stances of France political elite in 2012 and then the swift transition to a robust military operation early 2013. It also critically reflects on the various perceptions of France operation in Mali.

IV.1.1. France Diplomatic Stances and Rhetoric of Non-Intervention

To begin with, many perceive France as a country of 'pacifists' refraining to involve into military operation beyond its borders (Blanquer, 2013; Francis, 2013). However, this view misses the mark of specific France relations with its former colonies especially in Francophone Africa. The label Francafrique coined by President Houphouet Boigny in 1955 relate to an overarching set of secret agreements, controversial commercial deals as well as underground political networks crafting France pré-carré in Francophone post-colonial Africa (Lussato and Halifa-Legrand, 2011). That justify the observation that 'France wields a level of influence in sub-Saharan Africa that it cannot command anywhere else in the world' (Melly and Darracq, 2013). France sphere d'influence and working methods in Africa is summarized by the words of Sarkozy's secretary-general of presidency who asserted that 'we're not going to fall out with those who do us great service' (Boisbouvier, 2010).

It is attention-grabbing that rebellion in Northern Mali triggered in 2012, in the midst of France presidential elections between Nicolas Sarkozy and Francois Hollande. Of course, Mali issues became a point of contention between the candidates. During the live presidential debate in May 2012, both Sarkozy and Hollande seemed to agree that the threat in Mali was the Islamists and that France needed to step up its involvements in order to help rescue destabilized Mali. However, when it comes to the nature and the level of the help, nothing was clear[39].

---

[39] The debate between Nicolas Sarkozy and Francois Hollande is accessible on Le Monde at http://www.lemonde.fr/election-presidentielle-2012/article/2012/05/03/compte-rendu-integral-du-debat-nucleaire-institutions-politique-etrangere-partie-5_1694483_1471069.html and Xinhua article on MaliJet 'Mali : la France condamne à nouveau le renversement de l'ordre constitutionnel' at

Under Sarkozy, from January until April 2012, France did nothing more than discouraging French citizen to visit Northern Mali in November 2011 given the Islamist threats and later condemning the coup against ATT regime in April 2012[40]. It is curious that Sarkozy who led previous campaigns in Lybia on 2011 on the ground of humanitarian interventions and protection of civilians refrained to do so in the case of Mali. Barluet (2012) reported, using Francafrique jargon, that ATT was perceived as a 'bad student' in France because of his tiny efforts to fight terrorist in the Sahel and weedy cooperation with Paris[41]. Sarkozy government subsequently advised French citizens to leave Mali triggering critics within French Congress that Paris was abandoning its 'responsibilities' in Sub-Saharan Africa[42].

When Hollande took over the power in May 2012 on the promise of 'rupture' with Francafrique, he first avoided to discuss prospects of France intervening in Mali, stating that it was the role of Africa to do so. Thus, when Niger President Issoufou visited him in Paris on June 2012, he clearly said that 'if an intervention is decided upon, it's for the Africans to lead it' and that France will just back an African resolution at the UNSC (RFI, 2012). So, it was clear for France that military power could be used, but only by Africans with a logistical and financial support from Paris and others. There were even reports that France

---

http://www.malijet.com/actualite-politique-au-mali/flash-info/40766-mali-la-france-condamne-a-nouveau-le-renversement-de-l-ordre-con.html, accessed June 2014.

[40] See Paris Match article 'Mali. la France déconseille la destination' at
http://www.parismatch.com/Actu/International/Mali-La-France-deconseille-la-destination-158328, accessed June 2014.

[41] See Le Figaro article 'Paris tourne sans regrets la page du «mauvais élève» ATT' at
http://www.lefigaro.fr/international/2012/03/22/01003-20120322ARTFIG00755-paris-tourne-sans-regrets-la-page-du-mauvais-eleve-att.php, accessed June 2014.

[42] See Le Figaro article 'Paris conseille aux Français de quitter le Mali' at
http://www.lefigaro.fr/international/2012/04/02/01003-20120402ARTFIG00426-paris-conseille-au-francais-de-quitter-le-mali.php?pagination=3 and CRIDEM article 'France: Critiques au sujet de l'interdiction de se rendre au Sahel' at http://actu.cridem.org/archive/article/2011/57608, accessed June 2014.

could send drones in Mali to fight AQIM and its upshots with US and EU support (Hirsch, 2012).

This rhetoric of non-intervention was the leitmotiv of France diplomatic stances from June to December 2012. Accordingly, France Foreign minister Laurent Fabius insisted on July 2012 that 'France, for obvious reasons, cannot be on the frontline in Mali. It is up to Africans themselves to do so, in the framework of international law' because there is a risk of reactions against the former 'colonizer'[43]. Fabius was followed few months later by France Defense Minister, Jean Yves le Drian who stressed in an interview to BBC on November 2012 that France will only provide logistical support to an African mission without deploying its troops on the ground or in the air[44]. Francois Hollande later emphasized during a press conference that France will, in no case intervened itself in Mali crisis[45].

IV.1.2. Launch of Serval and France Maskirovka

On the other hand, on 20 December 2012, the UNSC passed the resolution 2085 which authorized 'the deployment of an African-led International Support Mission in Mali (AFISMA) for an initial period of one year'. The resolution was voted unanimously at the UNSC and Paris played a key role to facilitate its backing (Francis, 2013; Chrisafis, 2013).

---

[43] Laurent Fabius answers to Journalists questions on 12 July 2012 are available at http://www.diplomatie.gouv.fr/fr/le-ministre/laurent-fabius/presse-et-media-21596/article/entretien-du-ministre-des-affaires-100898, accessed June 2014.
[44] Jean-Yves Le Drian interview by BBC and subsequent article 'La France n'interviendra pas au Mali' at http://www.bbc.co.uk/afrique/region/2012/11/121113_mali_france_defense_minister.shtml, accessed June 2014.
[45] See RFI article 'Opération militaire au Mali : la France n'interviendra pas «elle-même»' at http://www.rfi.fr/afrique/20121113-operation-militaire-mali-france-interviendra-pas-elle-meme-union-africaine-addis-abeba-conseil-securite/, accessed June 2014.

Surprisingly, on 11 January 2013, France made a drastic U-turn and launched a fully-fledged military intervention in Northern Mali following a demand formulated two days earlier by Interim Mali President, Dioncounda Traore. France radical shift from its previous diplomatic stances was diversely appreciated. There was a lot of debate especially on its mandate and purpose and also speculations about its duration and France overall strategy.

According to the ICG (2013, p 17), there was a visible confusion and perceptible inconsistency in France communications 'about the nature, objectives and duration of the military intervention called Operation Serval'. For Francois Hollande, the aim was to stop Islamists progression towards Bamako while France Prime Minister, Jean Marc Ayrault thought that the goal was to clear the path for the deployment of the African forces of AFISMA in line with the burden-sharing doctrine and further, France Defense Minister settled that the ultimate goal was to reconquer Northern Mali from rebels (ICG, 2013).

This imbroglio about France operation Serval was reflected in analyses. For many, France military intervention purpose was to halt the progression of rebels towards Bamako, the Capital city of Mali and recapture Northern Mali on the ground of humanitarianism and global fight against Islamist terrorists (Boutelli and Williams, 2013; Francis, 2013). For others, France intervention was simply 'carved from colonialism' and a relic of Francafrique in a system of 'the Long Durée of Imperial Blowback' (Levine, 2013; Bergamaschi, 2013). Some also argued that France intervened to simply protect its geostrategic and economic interests in the country and the region (Elischer, 2013; AJCS, 2013). On the same line, Francis (2013) argues that France energy security was at stake and that the country intervened mainly to protect Areva Uranium plants in Niger which could have been affected by a spillover of the conflict. He further adds that France 'depend heavily on the uranium from its two uranium mines in

Niger' which are essential to consolidate France position as the 'largest exporter of electricity in the world' (Francis, 2013, p 7).

It can be added that France intervention also aimed at carving the country's position into ongoing oil exploration which started in Northern Mali since 2005 according to Think Security Africa. Another view is that Serval set the derivation for a definitive France presence in Mali (Haidara, 2014). This view is corroborated by the signature on July 2014 of a near-secret defense agreement between Mali and France with the controversial use of the Northern base of Tessalit.

Some analysts went on to question the legitimacy of France operation arguing that Serval was not mentioned in UNSC Resolution 2085 and that the request of Interim President Traore to Francois Hollande was invalid because it was not representing a government democratically elected (Nanga, 2013; Bergamaschi and Diawara, 2013). Furthermore, Bergamaschi (2013) states that beyond the rationale of protecting its African partner, the reference to an 'Islamist threat' was vital in legitimizing France intervention in the lens of the international community. Lawyers of the European Journal of International Law argue that the legality of Serval was meticulously constructed around self-reinforcing interpretations of the international law notably the collective self-defense under article 51 of the UN Charter, the consent of the Malian authorities and a broad interpretation of UNSC Resolution 2085 (Christakis and Bannelier, 2013). Hadzi-Vidanovic (2013) goes further and suggests that 'this hybrid approach certainly deserves attention and merits serious consideration in the future efforts to regulate controversial forms of armed intervention'. However, academics point out that Serval was specifically tailored to suit France military intervention into the Francophone space of West Africa and avoid the classic criticism of France intrusion into internal African Affairs (Bergamaschi and Diawara, 2013).

71

France overall strategy has also fueled debates. Specifically by which tactic the operation was planned behind the scenes, beyond the non-interventionism rhetoric of 2012. According to the ICG (2013), it is limpid that Serval was sudden but strategically planned long in advance. The ICG (2013) thinks that there two plans: a plan A consisting of France publicly advocating and working for the deployment of African forces of AFISMA and a plan B for a robust France intervention was planned in parallel. The ICG (2013) suggests that plan A failed because it meant that by the time African troops would have arrived in September 2013, the situation would have already quickly degenerated.

Other observers add insights to this proposition arguing that Serval had a secret story by way of France pulling the string in the background with the consent of Interim President, Dioncounda Traore (Jauvert and Halifa-Legrand, 2013). They suggest that the scenario for Serval was specifically ordered by President Hollande in case the Islamists moved southward to thwart AFISMA deployment (Jauvert and Halifa-Legrand, 2013). They also submit that there was collusion based on a win-win strategy between the rebels and an important fraction of the militaries in Bamako led by the coup leader, Sanogo (Jauvert and Halifa-Legrand, 2013). For them, the rebels did not intend to seize Bamako but the key town of Sévaré and its strategic airport which could serve for the deployment of AFISMA (Jauvert and Halifa-Legrand, 2013). Jauvert and Halifa-Legrand (2013) propose that once Sévaré was taken, Sanogo and its supports could easily claim that Interim President Dioncounda was incompetent and topple his government in order to craft one that will service the junta. On the same line, it is revealed that on 6 January 2013, France intelligence detected rebels' planning to move southward because they believed France will not intervene directly since President Hollande denied Central African Republic request to intervene in the country few days earlier (Jauvert and Halifa-Legrand, 2013). They were all surprised by the swift deployment of Serval and Sanogo supported the operation.

Similarly, Touchard (2014) adds that the seizure of Sévaré could have provided an upper-hand to rebels during a possible peace deal with Bamako and the international actors. Touchard (2014) thinks that France has turned into an expert in the art of military ruse and he argues that French militaries mastered the Russian notion of 'maskirovka' to mislead the rebels that it will not intervene while Serval concept of operations was ready-made.

IV.1.3. Assessment of the Reactions to France Operation in Mali

More often, France operation was acclaimed locally and internationally. According to Bergamaschi (2013), Captain Sanogo who previously rebuffed external intervention and interim authorities immediately approved it and framed it as the "least bad" scenario to reconquer Mali territorial integrity. President Issoufou of neighboring Niger was also keen to proclaim that Serval was the 'most popular of all French interventions in Africa' (Bergamaschi, 2013).

Indeed, Serval was officially backed by the ECOWAS and the AU after its launch by the AUPSC Report on its activities and the state of Peace and Security in Africa on 27 January 2013 which 'expressed its gratitude' to the country. In Europe, France was admired for its dauntless and swift move into a protracted Malian crisis. For example, Schmitz (2014) put that, as the sole willing and able European Military force, France deserved to be respected. He argued that France might be 'timid when it comes to economic reforms' but it is rather limpid that the country remains a bold 'grand nation when it comes to foreign policy ambitions' (Schmitz, 2014).

For Riondel, an analyst on Morocco World News, the success of Serval irritates Algerian generals who are reaping the fruits of their endless procrastination and internal rivalries (2013).

In Washington, France move met considerable support and reports emphasized that Serval role should focus on stopping the Islamists advances with a specific emphasis on US logistical and intelligence support to the country. Gibbs (2013) recounts the headlines of the Washington Post and the Wall Street Journal which respectively wrote that 'France comes to the rescue of Mali' and 'The White House scotches Pentagon plans to help the French'.

Delaporte (2013) rushed to draw lessons learned from France intervention suggesting that a 'new type of ad hoc international coalition — especially in the air' could be derived from Serval based on the watchwords 'Fight Alone, Supply Together'. Delaporte (2013) later reported France Chief of Staff, Amiral Guillaud stating that Serval used a new 'Golden rule' for French operations 'First to enter, and first to leave the theater' of operation to 'avoid a solely and long-lasting national military involvement'. However, Guillaud statement is contradicted by the transformation of Serval into Barkane and the signature of military agreements between France and Mali on July 2014 which consolidate France military presence in Mali and the region.

Batou (2013) thinks that this intervention propelled France strategic influence in Mali at the expense of its 'western and Chinese competitors'. He adds that the operation was codenamed Serval to mimic a cat 'able to urinate twenty times per hour to mark his territory' and that it signals France renewed appetite for African resources and the revival of France 'imperialism' to regain its clout in the region (Batou, 2013).

Detractors of Serval were few. There was of course the classic discourse emanating mostly from Africa about France imperialism and neo-colonialist politics which facilitated the intervention of France in its former African colony only to secure its latest sphere d'influence (Batou, 2013; Nanga, 2013; Elbinawi, 2013). Milne (2013) reflected that Serval was a spillover blowback from NATO military intervention in Libya and that France operation Mali would also lead to impending blowbacks for the country.

There were also accounts of France using the success of Serval for commercial gains that is to sell France's Rafale fighter to the 'United Arab Emirates and possibly elsewhere' (Gibbs, 2013). Interestingly, Qatar, a former ally of France in Libya, indirectly thrown stone on Serval through its Al Jazeera Center for Studies (AJCS) arguing that Serval was 'the first real setback for' President Hollande who was shifting back to the politics of Francafrique (AJCS, 2013). The AJCS also claimed that Serval could draw France and its African allies into an AZAWAD quagmire like in Somalia (AJCS, 2013). AJCS (2013) seems also to side with Touaregs and Arabs when it claims that France supported and trained 'militias with ethnic links to the Songhai' which could revive the 'racial and ethnic dimensions' detrimental mostly to the first which have already suffered a lot according to the article.

AJCS bias is quickly put into perspective when Ping (2014) argues that Qatar was present in Mali since 'end of June 2012 in Gao' and that the country financed MUJAO Islamists according to France intelligence. Another account of AJCS partiality stems from perceptions in Mali that France protected the Touaregs and Arabs of the MNLA instead of disarming their militias (Assadeck, 2012; Schneider, 2013)46. There were also accounts that France denied Mali

---

[46] See also MALIJET article 'Deal entre la France et le Mnla' at http://www.malijet.com/actualte_dans_les_regions_du_mali/rebellion_au_nord_du_mali/93695-deal-entre-la-france-et-le-mnla.html, accessed June 2014.

army to enter Kidal after it was retaken from rebels and MNLA militias were still controlling the city (Sylla, 2013; Dao, 2013).

In fact, the general thinking in Mali was that France and MNLA concluded a deal so the first could equip the other to fight terrorists within its space and the other will make sure that Mali army never returned to Kidal (Assadeck, 2012; Sylla, 2013; Dao, 2013)[47]. Ledoux (2013) even suggests that France unproven deal with MNLA was motivated by the discovery of an important Uranium deposit in Kidal region under ATT regime that France intended to control absolutely. They were also reports that bullets found in dead bodies of Malian soldiers shot by the MNLA were the same used by France Special Forces (Sow, 2014). However, this argumentation requires further investigation for the reason that France could always secure Uranium deal without castrating Mali control on Kidal since the country fits into France traditional sphere d'influence.

In France, There are accounts that the country military leadership was eager to involve troops in Mali to impress the public opinion and to circumvent defense and specifically OPEX budget cuts in a time of severe economic crisis (Roy 2013; Gibbs, 2013).

Whatever the case, Serval helped substantially to quickly weaken and push back the Islamists into their caverns deep in the Sahara desert. President Hollande was welcomed as a 'hero' in Bamako on 02 February 2013 and he did not fell to recall during his speech that France stood with Mali 'not to serve any particular interest'. Further Hollande was awarded UNESCO peace prize for his intervention which secured the world heritage of Timbuktu on June 2013. Most importantly, Serval key outcome was the signature of an undisclosed military agreement on 16 July 2014 between France and Mali that underpins France

---

[47] See also MALIWEB article 'Après l'accord de Ouaga : La France interdit Kidal à Didier et à Gamou' at http://www.maliweb.net/armee/apres-laccord-de-ouaga-la-france-interdit-kidal-a-didier-et-a-gamou-155194.html, accessed June 2014.

presence in the region. This agreement is a stronger replacement of the previous accord of military technical assistance of 1985 between both countries. According to France defense Minister Jean-Yves Le Drian, this agreement signals the commencement of a new era of defense cooperation between France and Mali which chosen to rely on its former colonial master for its security, notwithstanding the APSA and its 'African solutions to African problems' adage.

It is interesting to harness that Cote d'Ivoire, a key ECOWAS and AU member state, adopted few days before Mali, a new defense agreement with France. When one connect the dots, this series of defense agreement between France and its former colonies prove in the words of Wyss (2013) that 'the gendarme stays in Africa' and intends to consolidate its pré-carré. This logic of bilateral security agreements stands in stark contrast with UN growing doctrine of 'burdern-sharing' between multilateral partners when it comes to security in Africa and beyond. Still, it raises troubling set of interrogations about the APSA, especially its capability and reliability and put simply the level of trust of African political elites into the continental peace and security architecture. The next part assesses ECOWAS-AU axis and its strategy to address Mali crisis.

IV.2. Appraisal of APSA in Mali Crisis: In the Intricacy of ECOWAS-AU Axis

Mali protracted crisis embodied at its height between 2012 and 2013 a set of complex dynamics which required sub-local, sub-regional and continental attention. This section intends to assess the intricacy of ECOWAS-AU axis in light on three interrelated dynamics specifically the mediation of ECOWAS and the AU within the APSA, the sub-local forces at work particularly the 'pays du champ' initiative and finally the va-t-en guerre perspective from MICEMA to AFISMA.

IV.2.1. Regional Mediation in Mali: Dynamics of ECOWAS-AU Axis within the APSA

Since its entry into force in 2008, the Memorandum of Understanding between the African Union and the RECs entrust the primary role in the promotion and maintenance of peace, security and stability in Africa to the AU (article 20.1). Besides, it corroborates RECs comparative advantages and encourages them to anticipate and prevent conflicts within and among their member states including through peacemaking and the deployment of peace support missions (article 20.1). It also seals APSA principle of complementarity by which AU and the RECs should ensure a regular exchange of information and build up synergies through interlinked mechanisms and joint activities with efforts of vertical and horizontal coordination at the level of AU (article 15).

In the case of Western Africa, the ECOWAS established earlier in 1999, a Mechanism for Conflict Prevention, Management, Resolution, Peace-keeping and Security (MCPMRPS) which made the organization a forerunner in the management of peace and security on the continent. Therefore, Mali as a founding member of the ECOWAS and the AU has seen APSA mechanisms and specifically the axis ECOWAS-AU taking the lead in addressing its crisis.

There is the argument that ECOWAS and the APSA early warning systems were impotent or slow to identify preliminary signs of Mali crisis; and thus ECOWAS and the AU failed to take any preventive measure to address the crisis at its onset (Sambe, 2012; Attakpah, 2012). For Attakpah (2012), ECOWAS Early Warning System is 'grossly inadequate' and 'did nothing to help Mali to counter the advance of the rebels'.

However, this view is challenged by the fact that at the onset of the crisis, ECOWAS diplomats led by Albert Tevoedjre visited President ATT of Mali on February 2012. The goal of the visit was to make inquiries about the situation in Northern Mali where the coalition of rebels had attacked and captured the city of Menaka (Tine, 2012). During their audience with President ATT, he downplayed the crisis arguing that it was simply an internal problem created by a minority group using fear to agitate people in the country (Tine, 2012).

Conversely, Tine (2012) puts that ECOWAS diplomatic move was flawed because it targeted only the government without including the armed groups. It could be one of the reasons Mali could not receive the necessary support from ECOWAS to put up with the spillover of the rebels southward and the coup d'état against ATT regime (Tine, 2012). According to the representative of ECOWAS in Mali, Chéacka Aboudou Toure, ECOWAS warned president ATT of a probable coup against his regime[48]. So, ATT regime seems to have ignored or minimized ECOWAS warnings. In any case, Mali crisis has been high on the agenda of ECOWAS since its commencement.

At the AU, Mali crisis was given a second-class priority at its beginning, because of degenerating problem of food insecurity in the Sahel in early 2012[49]. At the time, Mali was a member of the AUPSC and its delegates surely echoed ATT perceptions that the northern crisis was an in-house matter that the government will quickly take care of. Consequently, the Report of the Peace and Security Council on its Activities and the State of Peace and Security in Africa released on 30 January 2012 did not mention the crisis in Mali while the

---

[48] The representative of ECOWAS in Mali, Chéacka Aboudou Toure hosted on 28 May 2013 a communication on the architecture of peace and security of ECOWAS. Watch it in French at https://www.youtube.com/watch?v=m_Qk-7JIF8k, accessed June 2014.

[49] Check 2012 AUPSC Agenda, Communiqués and Reports at www.peaceau.org, accessed June 2014.

rebels were already controlling some cities in the country's north[50]. Unpredictably, the assembly decision theoretically based on that report recognized that the proliferation of weapons in the Sahelo-Saharan region was a risk for 'long-term security and stability' of Mali and strongly condemned the activities of the armed group in Northern Mali. AU decision was surely guided by assertive ECOWAS move at the onset of the crisis.

The AU was apprehensive about the situation in Northern Mali but its unawareness of the complexity and scale of the crisis was uncovered when the organization naively organized a ministerial meeting of the Peace and Security Council in Bamako on 20 March 2012, the dawn of the coup against ATT regime[51]. The meeting agenda was the challenges faced by the Sahel region namely the drought in North Mali and the resulting afflux of hopeless refugees. Surprised by the swift collapse of ATT regime, AU has to negotiate with the coup leaders for the safe evacuation of its diplomats. Thus, AU Chairperson, Jean Ping had to set-up a Crisis Management Team, which worked timelessly to secure the safe evacuation of its diplomats namely Foreign Affairs Ministers of Kenya and Zimbabwe, H.E. Mr. Moses Wetangula and H.E. Mr. Simbarashe Mumbengegwi, respectively[52].

This clearly pinpoints that the vertical coordination between the AU and ECOWAS was botched at this level since ECOWAS representative in Mali,

---

[50] Download the Report of the Peace and Security Council on its Activities and the State of Peace and Security in Africa released on 30 January 2012 at http://www.peaceau.org/uploads/assembly-au-6-xviii-e.pdf, accessed June 2014.

[51] Read the Press Release setting the date of that specific AUPSC Meeting 'The African Union concerned by the situation in the Sahel Ministerial meeting of the AU Peace and Security Council in Bamako' at http://www.peaceau.org/en/article/the-african-union-concerned-by-the-situation-in-the-sahel-ministerial-meeting-of-the-au-peace-and-security-council-in-bamako#sthash.f59ROlaV.dpuf, accessed June 2014.

[52] AU Secures the Evacuation from Mali of FA Ministers of Kenya and Zimbabwe - See more at: http://www.peaceau.org/en/article/au-secures-the-evacuation-from-mali-of-fa-ministers-of-kenya-and-zimbabwe#sthash.BsC9Wsx8.dpuf, accessed June 2014.

Aboudou Toure admits in 2013 that his organization was aware of the coup and even its date[53].

At the crisis height, President Yayi Boni of Benin, a key member of ECOWAS was also the President of the AU. On 18 February 2012, he invited the RECs presidents to an ad-hoc summit in Cotonou in order to learn from their experiences and elaborate a roadmap for his mandate during his leadership as the Chair of the AU[54]. But, it can be argued that he was not assertive enough to conciliate the position of the AU and the ECOWAS on Mali crisis and was simply outweighed by Burkina Faso and Cote d'Ivoire during the mediation process in Mali.

Another point of contention is that President Boni energies were chiefly directed to unravel the protracted race for the position of Chairperson of the AUC. Indeed, the AU was crippled from January to July 2012 by a lengthy leadership competition between Jean Ping of Gabon and Dlamini-Zuma of South Africa. This resulted in a power vacuum in the organization and President Boni appeared more concerned about the power struggle at the AUC than the Mali crisis. So, on 17 March 2012, he received again African leaders in Cotonou to resolve the deadlock at the head of the AUC and Mali crisis was not on the agenda while the rebels were already in control of large parts of the country and the coup d'état against ATT regime was a matter of days.

After the coup against ATT regime, ECOWAS was swift to condemn it and held an emergency summit in Abidjan, on 27 March 2012. The outcome was a communiqué released on 29 March suspending Mali membership and demanding the restoration of constitutional order in the country as well as assets

---

[53] Ibid, 49.
[54] President Yayi Boni organized a Mini Summit of the AU at Cotonou on 18 February 2012. Watch his speech at https://www.youtube.com/watch?v=GWY-j-CzrMg, accessed June 2014.

freeze and border to weaken and isolate the junta[55]. ECOWAS also appointed President Blaise Compaoré of Burkina Faso as its mediator in Mali and decided to dispatch a high-level delegation to Mali to acquaint the mutineers with the content of Summit decisions and to discuss, in particular, the modalities for the speedy restoration of constitutional order in Mali[56].

Vines (2013), Weiss and Welz (2014) argue that there was a mismatch in the pace of ECOWAS and AU to condemn the coup and suspend Mali. Vines (2013) specifically puts that 'ECOWAS was weeks ahead in suspending Mali from its membership and calling for action'.

This argument is put into question for the reason that the AU condemned Mali coup the same day in a press release calling explicitly for the respect of constitutional order in Mali[57]. The next day, the AU issued another press release condemning the action of the mutineers and reaffirming Africa's zero tolerance for any unconstitutional change of Government[58]. AU decisively suspended Mali membership during its PSC meeting on 23 March 2012, two days after the coup and almost a week before ECOWAS decision, in stark contradiction with Vines argument[59]. More importantly, the decision expressed its appreciation of

---

[55] The communiqué of ECOWAS emergency mini-summit and its decisions are available online at http://news.ecowas.int/presseshow.php?nb=092&lang=en&annee=2012, accessed June 2014.

[56] Ibid,.

[57] The African Union calls for the respect of constitutional order in Mali - See more at: http://www.peaceau.org/en/article/the-african-union-calls-for-the-respect-of-constitutional-order-in-mali#sthash.FwgFlrcl.dpuf, accessed June 2014.

[58] The African Union strongly condemns the action of the mutineers who announced that they have taken power in Mali - See more at: http://www.peaceau.org/en/article/the-african-union-strongly-condemns-the-action-of-the-mutineers-who-announced-that-they-have-taken-power-in-mali#sthash.zMZXBDVO.dpuf, accessed June 2014.

[59] The Peace and Security Council of the African Union (AU), at its 315th meeting, held in Addis Ababa on 23 March 2012, adopted the following decision on the situation in the Republic of Mali - See more at: http://www.peaceau.org/en/article/the-peace-and-security-council-of-the-african-union-au-at-its-315th-meeting-held-in-addis-ababa-on-23-march-2012-adopted-the-following-decision-on-the-situation-in-the-republic-of-mali#sthash.G7TZnX48.dpuf, accessed June 2014.

ECOWAS efforts and the deliberation took place in the presence of the ECOWAS representative who briefed the PSC on Mali situation. Another interesting fact is that, ECOWAS meeting held almost a week later in accordance with the spirit of APSA decided to transmit its decisions, namely the suspension of Mali, to the AUPSC for information and action[60]. This is a case of vibrant collaboration between the AU and ECOWAS.

However, it appears that there was confusion about the organization leading the mediation in Mali within the APSA. This intricacy was evidenced when the AU established on 20 March 2012 a support and follow-up group to mediate the crisis under its aegis and the United Nations, comprising all the neighboring countries, the relevant Regional Economic Communities (ECOWAS and the Community of the Sahelo-Saharan States – CEN-SAD), as well as the international partners concerned[61]. The AU seemed to concede only a second role to ECOWAS while it was well-known that CEN-SAD was not functional following the demise of Gaddafi regime. The PSC Communiqué released two days later tended to rectify that and conferred ECOWAS a more strategic position in the mediation. It stated that 'in consultation with ECOWAS and the UN' the AUC must take all necessary measure to step up the support and follow-up group on Mali crisis[62].

The damage has already been done because a week later, ECOWAS decided to organize its own mediation and Burkina Faso was chosen to facilitate the

---

[60] Last paragraph of the communiqué issued by ECOWAS emergency mini-summit at: http://news.ecowas.int/presseshow.php?nb=092&lang=en&annee=2012, accessed June 2014.
[61] 314th Meeting of the Peace and Security Council at Ministerial level - See more at: http://www.peaceau.org/en/article/314th-meeting-of-the-peace-and-security-council-at-ministerial-level#sthash.elEdKnWz.dpuf, accessed June 2014.
[62] The Peace and Security Council of the African Union (AU), at its 315th meeting, held in Addis Ababa on 23 March 2012, adopted the following decision on the situation in the Republic of Mali - See more at: http://www.peaceau.org/en/article/the-peace-and-security-council-of-the-african-union-au-at-its-315th-meeting-held-in-addis-ababa-on-23-march-2012-adopted-the-following-decision-on-the-situation-in-the-republic-of-mali#sthash.G7TZnX48.dpuf, accessed June 2014.

process. Furthermore, ECOWAS decided to set up a high delegation constituted of six heads of states that will officially visit Mali on 29 March and acquaint the Junta with the content of its decision and the modalities for the speedy restoration of constitutional order in Mali[63]. This can be interpreted as a lack of strategic coordination between the AU and ECOWAS or conversely, it can be conceded that the AU intended to enlarge the scope of the mediation by opening up space for the UN and other partners to participate in the process while enabling ECOWAS to act swiftly.

Decisively, ECOWAS was the first institution to send a delegation to Mali to mediate Mali crisis. On 29 March 2012, ECOWAS then president, Alassane Ouattara flew to Bamako but couldn't land because protesters had occupied the airport. The visit of ECOWAS delegation was canceled and the presidents decided to meet the next day in Abidjan to assess the situation and take appropriate measures. After Abidjan meeting, ECOWAS took harsh measures on 31 March against the junta and its CNRDRE specifically diplomatic, economic and financial sanctions with assets freeze of officials and their associates and the closing of ECOWAS seaports to landlocked Mali.

According to ICG (2012), these sanctions had an immediate impact on the junta who decided to sign with ECOWAS mediators on 6 April 2012 a framework agreement providing a series of steps for the restoration of constitutional order in Mali. This was perceived as an important achievement for ECOWAS because the coup leaders accepted to relinquish power in less than ten days, a record in Africa according to ECOWAS representative in Mali, Aboudou Touré.

However, the ICG (2012, p 22) points out that the junta did not really relinquish power but the agreement provided the CNRDRE a 'role' and 'place' in the

---

[63] Read the communiqué issued by ECOWAS emergency mini-summit at:
http://news.ecowas.int/presseshow.php?nb=092&lang=en&annee=2012, accessed June 2014.

transitional process. In fact, the CNRDRE signed the framework agreement on behalf of Mali without the consultation of the country's political class opening a space for it to control the transition process.

Anyhow, the agreement provided for the president of National Assembly, Dioncounda Traore to step up as the new president of Mali for forty days and officially replace overthrown ATT. ATT on his side released a statement before the signature of the agreement to acknowledge ECOWAS decision, officially resign and open the space for Dioncounda Traoré to lead the forty days transition. The agreement was welcomed by the AUPSC during its meeting on 12 April 2012 and the AU promised to accompany the implementation process of the Framework Agreement in the dynamic of APSA.

Dioncounda Traoré, in charge of the transition had to form a government to handle the period. Yet, ICG (2012, p 22) suggests that 'Traoré had no input' on the choice of Cheick Modibo Diarra as the Prime Minister of the transitional government in the terms of the Framework Agreement. For the ICG (2012, p 23), Diarra was imposed to Traoré by the CNRDRE with the blessing of Djibril Bassolé of Burkina Faso, ECOWAS mediator. In fact, Marchal (2012) suggests that Diarra is a 'good friend' of Blaise Compaoré, the President of Burkina-Faso and lead mediator of Mali crisis. Marchal proposition is confirmed by the fact that Diarra is an executive of the International Council for Solidarity with Burkina Faso, a platform established by President Compaoré to promote his country worldwide[64]. In addition, President Compaoré 'managed to get one his henchmen, Sadio Lamine Sow, appointed as minister of foreign affairs' in Mali transitional government (Marchal, 2012, p 6).

Certainly, the ECOWAS mediator, Burkina-Faso president sought to influence the transition in Mali but he was not the only one. Marchal (2012) observes that

---

[64] See CISAB website at www.cisab.org/index.php?page=cisab&article=1, accessed June 2014.

ECOWAS chair, President Ouattara of Côte d'Ivoire managed to get Hamidoun Touré appointed as Mali minister of the communication and official spokesperson. Hamidoun Touré served as the spokesperson for the United Nations Operation in Côte d'Ivoire (UNOCI) which helped to consolidate Ouattara power in Cote d'Ivoire. Therefore, ECOWAS mediation was biased and vividly criticized by analysts (ICG, 2012; Marchal, 2012; Lecocq et al., 2012).

Furthermore, there were reports that Burkina-Faso was colliding with the MNLA through the support of France specifically providing weapons and sophisticated equipments to the rebels (Guindo and Tiékorobani, 2012). According to Mali Actu, MNLA leader, Bilal Ag Chérif was rescued by Burkina Faso army and transferred to Ouagadougou after his Islamists allies chased the MNLA in Gao[65]. This can be interpreted as an effort by Burkina-Faso to secure the availability of credible negotiators within the rebellion.

Anyway, Burkina-Faso and Cote d'Ivoire weaken ECOWAS mediation as they were pushing their own agenda in Mali transition. Sanogo and the junta surfed on these shortcomings to set Mali public opinion against ECOWAS and Burkina-Faso mediation. Guindo and Tiékorobani (2012) for example recall that Mali and Burkina-Faso fought two times in 1974 and 1984 over Agacher strip which fell aftermath largely under Mali authority.

The CNRDRE rallied its supporters under the umbrella of COPAM who specifically set a 'panafricanist' agenda to counter ECOWAS mediation into Mali crisis. During its first appearance on 08 April 2012, COPAM managed to rally large parts of Bamako radical 'patriotic' figures from the far right and set its agenda against the leadership of Dioncouda Traoré seen as an extension of

---

[65] See 'Le président du MNLA évacué par l'armée burkinabè' at http://maliactu.net/le-president-du-mnla-evacue-par-larmee-burkinabe/, accessed June 2014.

ATT regime[66]. COPAM also played the nationalist card to rally important among of 'youth with no jobs or education and vindictive military elements whose common enemy was the old Malian elites and foreign actors' (ICG, 2012, p 21). COPAM claims of pan Africanism are essentially baseless since it opposed vehemently all the deed of institutions epitomizing the pan African paradigm specifically ECOWAS. Still, that argument rallied crowd of misinformed young who manifested at many occasions to support the group. It can be said that COPAM became popular because of external intervention in Cote d'Ivoire and Libya which spread belief among African elites that foreign intervention into an African state was surely subjective and disserving local interests (Lath, 2012).

However, it is justified to argue with Lecocq et al. (2012, p 14) that COPAM was a potentially 'dangerous' body. In fact, after ECOWAS meeting on 26 April 2012 that extended for one year the mandate of Dioncouda Traoré and the transitional government, the 70 year old man was assaulted in his office on 21 May by a mob allegedly connected to Sanogo and the CNRDRE. He was transferred to France for medical treatment and returned to Mali on 27 July 2012.

In this power vacuum, Sanogo, the coup leader was granted the status of Mali former head of state by Burkina-Faso foreign Minister, Djibril Bassolé acting as ECOWAS mediator. ECOWAS finally revoked the decision at its summits in June 2012 but it exposed the contradiction within the mediation process and ECOWAS approach to conduct a strong and fair mediation process in Mali.

This 'series of blunders and mistakes committed by mediators' can be justified by the abandon of regional leadership by Nigeria, the largest and strongest

---

[66] See the article 'Accord cadre entre le Cnrdre et la Cedeao / La Copam se prononce' at http://www.malijet.com/a_la_une_du_mali/41761-accord_cadre_entre_le_se_proponce.html, accessed June 2014.

ECOWAS member state which seemed to be busy with its internal Boko Haram terrorists (ICG, 2012, p 5). There is also the argument that Mali crisis was perceived as a 'francophone Africa' affair that could not affect directly English speaking countries (Helly and Rocca, 2013). These authors pursue that Dlamini-Zuma beginning at the AUC at the end of July 2012 did not ease AU relation with the ECOWAS because of mistrust about her 'South African agenda within the AU' (Helly and Rocca, 2013, p 4).

The role of Mali northern neighbors, specifically Algeria and Mauritania in certain aspects provides another lens to assess critically the involvement of AU and ECOWAS to unravel Mali crisis.

IV.2.2. The 'Pays du Champs' or 'Core' countries Effect: Mali Crisis in Algeria and Mauritania lenses

Algeria, Mali, Mauritania and Niger are members of the so-called 'pays du champs' or 'core' countries which are a group of states which decided to unite their forces against AQIM and other terrorist and transnational criminal activities in the Sahel. As Algerian Minister Abdelkader Messahel put it, the 'core' countries intend to consolidate and drive their own agenda in the Sahel against terrorism and transnational organized crime[67].

It is important to recall that the 'core' countries met in Bamako on 21 May 2011 and decided to put in place within eighteen months a joint intervention force capable to effectively deploy from 25.000 to 150.000 troops depending on the

---

[67] See La Nouvelle Republique article 'La coopération étrangère avec les «pays du champ» au menu' www.lnr-dz.com/index.php?page=details&id=4311, accessed July 2014.

importance of a given operation[68]. However, this initiative which could have prevented the formation of the rebellion in Northern Mali never came to life.

In fact Algeria, the most powerful Mali neighbor, is seen as counter-terrorist state and has been the key mediator of previous Northern Mali crisis especially Touareg rebellions of 1995 and 2009 (Arieff, 2012). In this vein, the country efforts climaxed with the setting of the 'Tamanrasset Plan' which led to the establishment of the Joint Military Operations Center (CEMOC) and the Joint Intelligence Center (JIC) in 2010 (Arieff, 2012). The CEMOC was supposed to organize joint exercise between Algeria, Niger, Mali, and Mauritania in order to coordinate 'regional response to cross-border terrorism, smuggling, and other armed group activity in the Sahel's vast and under-policed border regions' (Arieff, 2012). Yet, Mali crisis has proven that the CEMOC and the Joint Intelligence Center are empty shells whose efficiency remains unproven (Arieff, 2012).

One could also points that following AU 2002 Plan of Action, it was established in 2004 the African Centre for the Study and Research on Terrorism (ACSRT) based in Algiers to serve as a structure for centralizing information, studies and analyses on terrorism and terrorist groups and to develop Counter-Terrorism capacity building programs. However, the ACSRT was one of the main Achilles' heel of APSA and did not release any comprehensive study on Mali terrorists group nor proposed a strategy to tackle Mali crisis.

Algeria representatives were present to most ECOWAS and AU meetings but the country's position evolved slowly during 2012 aside from rejecting MNLA declaration of independence. However, Alegria, considered the strongest and most capable Mali neighbor in terms of experience with Islamist rebellions as

[68] See Jeune Afrique article 'Lutte anti-Aqmi : les "pays du champs" en conclave à Bamako' at www.jeuneafrique.com/Article/ARTJAWEB20110521101945/algerie-france-diplomatie-niger-mali-lutte-anti-aqmi-les-pays-du-champs-en-conclave-a-bamako.html, accessed July 2014.

well as 'unmatched military and intelligence resources' in the region was reluctant to back any plan of military intervention in Mali (Gearan, 2012).

Many suggest that Algiers stance stemmed from the uneven relations it entertained with ATT regime (Lacher, 2012; Wing, 2012; Arieff, 2012). Wing (2012) reminds that Algeria recalled its ambassadors from Mali in February 2010 after a French hostage was released by AQIM allegedly in exchange of AQIM prisoners from ATT regime. Arieff (2012) adds that Algerian-Malian relations were 'particularly troubled' under ATT regime because Mali was not sufficiently dedicated to eradicate AQIM and even colluded with the terrorist nebula.

There is also the argument that Algiers refrained to endorse ECOWAS plans since it is not a member of the organization (Lacher, 2012). The scholar pursue that Algiers was skeptical of Burkina-Faso mediation and specially the 'role of the Burkinabé President Blaise Compaoré in northern Mali' (Lacher, 2012). In fact, reports suggest that Algiers negotiated in parallel with radical Islamists of Ansar Dine notably Iyad Ag Ghali which is known to have been close to Algiers (Badibanga, 2012; Boitiaux, 2012). Anyway, Algiers was a fervent advocate of negotiations with some armed groups specially Ansar Dine.

The official justification advanced by President Bouteflika government was the constitutional principles of 'non- interference in the internal affairs of other states, rejection of violence as a means of settling conflicts, and the inviolability of borders inherited from the colonial era'[69] (Mesbah cited by Hamza, 2012). This posture can also stems from the doctrine that security in the sahel is solely

---

[69] Mohamed Shafik Mesbah, former senior officer at the Algerian intelligence service of DRS (Department of Intelligence and Security) was interviewed by Assiya Hamza of France 24. See subsequent article 'Can France and Algeria find common ground on Mali?' at http://www.france24.com/en/20121212-algeria-mali-france-common-ground-crisis-military-intervention/, accessed July 2014.

the business of the 'core' countries[70]. In fact, Algerian Interior Minister Daho Ould Kablia ruled out in 2011 that foreign powers could only provide intelligence, technology or training but cannot directly intervene in Algeria backyard[71].

Dockins (2013) thinks that being the wealthiest country and a natural leader in the region, Algeria was reluctant to any foreign intervention that might turn a space it considers its 'backyard' into a war zone (Dockins, 2013). Arieff (2012) states that Algiers was wary of ECOWAS intervention plan because the organization relied heavily on French technical and logistical capabilities which could degenerate into 'intelligence collection activities in the guise of assisting regional troops'.

However, after France took the lead by launching Serval, Algiers sought to assist and opened its airspace to French warplane operating in Mali on 13 January 2013. It was also a result of intense diplomatic lobbying and pressure on Algerian leadership by France and the USA notably the visit to Algiers of US Secretary of State Hillary Rodham Clinton on 29 October 2012 and her 'lengthy meeting with President Abdelaziz Bouteflika' (Gearan, 2012).

Algiers move met direct retaliation of AQIM-affiliated Mokhtar Belmokhtar battalion, the "Signers in Blood" who attacked In-Amena gas complex in Southern Algeria on 16 January 2013 and held more than 37 hostages, mostly European for four days before being crushed by Algeria counter-terrorism forces.

---

[70] See Algerie 1 article 'Ould Kablia et le terrorisme au Sahel: la sécurité apanage « exclusif » de quatre pays de la région' at www.algerie1.com/actualite/daho-ould-kablia-et-le-terrorisme-au-sahel-la-securite-apanage-exclusif-de-quatre-pays-de-la-region/, accessed July 2014.
[71] Ibid,.

On its side, Mauritania shares the longest border of Mali, over 2,300 km. In addition, it provides a closer access to Atlantic Ocean especially through the facilities of the Autonomous Port of Nouakchott. Furthermore, the country hosts a set of prominent MNLA leaders living as political refugee who harness the country's proximity to create a rear base in order to advance and promote MNLA agenda.[72]

Mauritania often had chilly relations with its southern neighbors of ECOWAS. The country withdrawal from the organization in 2000 was perceived as a 'black phobia' embedded in a 'deep identity crisis' as the country straddle 'on the cultural divide between black Africa and Arab North Africa' (Diallo, 2004). But, this one-dimensional view does not take into account the notion of space fluidity and cross-border threats facing Sahel states. Indeed, Mauritania participated to most of ECOWAS and AU meetings pertaining to Mali crisis in a bid to stress its view that a negotiated solution was the key to Mali crisis.

However, Mauritania has been very active on military counter-terrorist campaigns in 2010. Indeed, the Franco-Mauritanian raid against AQIM on July 2010 in Northern Mali in an attempt to help liberate a French hostage. The operation sparked harsh contestation in Mali about the violation of its territory[73]. Also the raid sidelined Algeria and 'ignored the regional security structures set up expressly to deal with AQIM' notably the 'core' countries initiatives including the CEMOC and JIC[74].

Mauritania military endeavors in Northern Mali on 2010 stands in direct contrast with the position taken by the country during Mali crisis of 2012.

---

[72] See for example the interview of Le Monde with Nina Wallet Intalou, a prominent women leader of the MNLA living in Nouakchott.

[73] See The Moor Next Door article 'RE: Franco-Mauritanian AQIM Raid' at http://themoornextdoor.wordpress.com/2010/08/01/re-franco-mauritanian-aqim-raid/, accessed July 2014.

[74] Ibid,.

Although, President Ould Abdel Aziz was a harsh critique of ATT regime specifically blaming him of laissez-faire against AQIM, the country framed its position against military intervention[75]. This stance could be motivated by the fear of the country to be embroiled in another military misadventure in Northern Mali territory following the failure of the hostage-rescue mission of 2010[76]. There is also the dread of the conflicts spillover over Mauritania largely porous borders with Mali.

Yet, Mauritania regime changed its posture after France launched operation Serval. During his press conference with Mauraitania President on January 2013, Francois Hollande insisted that 'Mauritania is ready to take its responsibilities vis-à-vis the terrorist threat should the Malian state issue such a request'[77]. That Mauritanian stance cannot be interpreted as a strong will to help its neighbor but rather a diplomatic formula crafted in face of a crumbling Malian state in need of a power epicenter to easily formulate such request. Furthermore, the country did not contribute a single soldier to AFISMA, a mission it considered an ECOWAS endeavor.

The 'pays du champs' or 'core' countries initiative came out to be a rigid structure to deal with Mali crisis, exposing its apathy for decisions taken in the framework of the APSA, specifically the va-t-en guerre standpoint of ECOWAS and the African Union.

---

[75] Newspaper Biladi reported in 2009 President Ould Abdel Aziz of Mauritania statement that 'as long as ATT remains in power, terrorism will not back down' in the region at http://www.rmibiladi.com/fr/images/pdf/biladifr416.pdf, accessed July 2014.

[76] The French hostage Michel Germaneau was executed by AQMI in retaliation for the commando operation for his release.

[77] Francois Hollande was cited in the Arabist article ' Mauritania's Society on the Mali War: Niet!! « Dekhnstan' at https://arabist.net/?offset=1358669183008, accessed July 2014.

IV.2.2. ECOWAS and AU va-t-en guerre Standpoint: From MICEMA to AFISMA

From the onset of Mali crisis in January 2012, ECOWAS has been at the fore front, standing for 'intervention in one of its most troubled member states' (Sandor, 2013). Surprisingly, from January to March 2012, the organization did not issue a single press release or communiqué on Mali. This could be explained by the power vacuum at the head of ECOWAS Commission stemming from the replacement of Ghanaian James Victor Gbeho by the Burkinabe Kadre Desire Ouedraogo. Also, that period saw the transition of the Chairmanship of the Authority of Heads of State and Government from President Goodluck Jonathan of Nigeria to President Alassane Dramane Ouattara of the Republic of Cote d'Ivoire.

However, while passing the torch to Ouedraogo, Gbeho recognized on 16 February 2012 that the resurgence of rebellion in Mali required urgent attention from the newly voted leadership[78]. Therefore, the new ECOWAS Commission Chair led the first fact-finding mission to the Republic of Mali from 16 to 18 March 2012. The mission issued a statement condemning 'the atrocities perpetrated in the north by the rebels, and [called] on the MNLA to immediately and unconditionally observe a cease-fire, lay down their weapons, and relinquish all occupied territory in the north to central authority'. ECOWAS then intended to launch a mediation process between the ATT regime and the rebels in order to settle the crisis peacefully.

Yet, three days after ECOWAS statement, ATT regime was overthrown by angry militaries complaining about the handling of the crisis in the north. While, the coup was unanimously condemned, ECOWAS communiqué from an

---

[78] See ECOWAS Press Release 'President Jonathan calls for stronger Ecowas unity, cohesion' at news.ecowas.int/presseshow.php?nb=021&lang=en&annee=2012, accessed July 2014.

emergency summit in Abidjan was the most stringent. It instructed 'the ECOWAS Commission to put the ECOWAS Standby Force on high alert for all eventualities' and informed the junta that 'ECOWAS shall take all necessary measures to re-establish constitutional order in Mali'. It was the basis of MICEMA (ECOWAS Mission in Mali).

The legal basis of ECOWAS standpoint germinates from the revised ECOWAS Treaty (1993) and the Mechanism for Conflict Prevention, Management, Resolution, Peace-Keeping and Security (1999) which put that 'intervention is required under circumstances of civil conflict that threaten to induce a humanitarian emergency or pose a significant threat to regional peace and security' (Sandor, 2013, p 3). But, ECOWAS stance alienated any attentive dialogue it could establish with Captain Sanogo, the junta chief. For example Sanogo was able to mobilize COPAM in order to persuade Bamako public opinion of the benefits of a new-fangled Panafricanism directed against ECOWAS.

All this deprived the organization from a valid interlocutor able to understand and impulse its vision towards a swift solution in Mali (Sandor, 2013; ICG, 2012). In this vein, an ECOWAS mission led by President Ouattara was denied landing at Bamako airport by a group of demonstrators as the organization was painted as an imperialist body in Bamako by COPAM and the junta.

On its side, the AU endorsed all ECOWAS decisions but did not officially embrace the discourse of military intervention even if it condemned the military coup. Moreover, AU established a Support and Follow up Group on the situation in Mali on March 2012 but the group held its first meeting four months later on 07 June 2012.

At the time Mali transitional institutions were put into place, there was a hope that it could stabilize Bamako and ease the dialogue with ECOWAS. Yet, the transition quickly displayed a lack of coordination arising from the presence of multiple centers of power in Bamako between the Captain Sanogo, President Dioncounda Traoré and the Prime Minister Diarra (Theroux-Benoni, 2013). Therefore, ECOWAS was unable to coordinate with Mali and MICEMA quickly reached deadlock when misunderstandings got high between ECOWAS defense chiefs and their Malian counterparts (ICG, 2012). ECOWAS was perceived as an 'arrogant' stakeholder by Sanogo and his followers (Theroux-Benoni, 2013). It is also argued that Sanogo and COPAM could muster public opinion against ECOWAS because of Cote d'Ivoire crisis of 2011 where the organization was perceived as 'weak' and/or 'complicit' of the stalemate (Lath, 2012).

ECOWAS was obliged to amend its demarche and sought an official request for intervention from Mali transition authorities. Thus, President Dioncounda Traoré formally requested ECOWAS military assistance on 05 September 2012. Yet, Mali demand was stained by flagrant inconsistencies notably on the role of ECOWAS troops on the ground[79]. This created confusion and ECOWAS asked for amendments of the request.

In effect, ECOWAS designed MICEMA to be a force of more than 3300 soldiers ready to engage in a military re-conquest of Northern Mali but the junta greatly contributed to throw out that baby with its bathwater. Analysts also put that MICEMA was condemned to death because it lacked 'practical basis of an intervention' especially crucial material and logistical support and 'capacity to engage in sustained counterinsurgency combat in both urban areas and desert terrain' (Sandor, 2013, p 2). Another reason MICEMA was abortive is the

---

[79] The junta had the unrealistic intention to battle alone for the re-conquest of Mali North while ECOWAS troops would be confined to protect the liberated cities.

denial by the UNSC on June 2012 to endorse ECOWAS request for international support despite the backing of the AUPSC.

Soon after its leadership crisis was solved, the AUC became more aggressive in seeking a solution to Mali crisis. Thus, in July 2012, the AUC took the lead in a bid to secure UNSC mandate and international support and also overcome the reluctance of the 'core' countries. It therefore reframed MICEMA into the more inclusive AFISMA, the African-led International Support Mission to Mali. A day after she took office, Nkosazana Dlamini-Zuma travelled to New York and agreed with ECOWAS that Mali crisis scope was beyond the region and needed for more AUC involvement[80].

The AUC dynamic invigorated the Support and Follow-up Group on the situation in Mali and the UNSC finally adopted on 21 December 2012, the resolution 2085 authorizing the deployment of AFISMA which was 'inspired by the Strategic Concept for the Resolution of the Crises in Mali and the harmonized Concept of Operations developed under the auspices of the AU'[81].

However, AU desire to benefit from the 'rapid implementation of a logistic support package funded by statutory contributions from the UN budget' was ignored by the UNSC and AFISMA implementation decelerated. In fact, it was clear that AU trusted that the UNSC will spearhead the financing of AFISMA[82]. So, it is no surprise that when France launched Serval, the AU and ECOWAS commended the operation and supported France action. France operation was a

---

[80] Watch the video 'Chairperson of the AUC Dr Nkosazana Dlamini Zuma in Mali' at https://www.youtube.com/watch?v=RhQ-Pq5a4Vg, accessed July 2014.

[81] See AU Press Release 'African Union welcomes the adoption by the Security Council of the United Nations of Resolution 2085 (2012) on Mali' at http://www.peaceau.org/en/article/african-union-welcomes-the-adoption-by-the-security-council-of-the-united-nations-of-resolution-2085-2012-on-mali#sthash.JDFuSNLa.dpuf, accessed July 2014.

[82] See Ambassador Ramtane Lamamra interview by AlQarra at 'L'Union Africaine compte sur l'ONU pour financer la MISMA' at https://www.youtube.com/watch?v=6N4qmEjLwtM, accessed July 2014.

clear reminder that AU and ECOWAS often display a 'rhetorical determination that goes beyond [their] capacity to deliver' swiftly without massive assistance of the UN and other partners (ICG, 2012, p 6).

Yet, the AU did not give up and the AFISMA decisively started to deploy at the end of January and Dlamini-Zuma appointed former President Pierre Buyoya as Special Representative and Head of the AFISMA. AU also sought to secure funding for AFISMA and organized in close consultation with ECOWAS, a donors' conference for AFISMA at its headquarters of Addis Ababa on 29 January 2013. The conference pledged 340 million euros for Mali and was a demonstration of Pan-African solidarity with countries like Sierra Leone or Namibia honoring their pledge of one million USD to help Mali recover.

AFISMA also provided a framework to integrate the huge Chadian contingent which was deployed to support Opération Serval. Chad has always pushed for an African-led military solution to Mali crisis[83] and its contingent was the backbone of France operation as its soldiers are accustomed to desert fierce battle styles and Chad army is able to sustain and accommodate death of its troops. However, Chad intervention on the side of France revived souvenir of world wars infamous 'Senegalese tirailleurs' fighting for their colonial master. So, the integration of Chad contingent into AFISMA helped clear that feeling.

The AUC did not spare its efforts and launched a series of initiative to foster security initiatives in the Sahel and beyond. Thus, it launched the 'Nouakchott process', with the goal to enhance security cooperation and the operationalization of the APSA in the Sahelo-Saharan region on 17 March 2013[84]. AU also crafted the African Capacity for Immediate Response to Crises

---

[83] See for example Jeune Afrique article 'Tchad - Idriss Déby Itno : "J'ai trop longtemps prêché dans le désert"' at http://www.jeuneafrique.com/Article/ARTJAWEB20120717104415/, accessed July 2014.
[84] See the first conclusion of the Ministerial meeting on the enhancement of security cooperation and the operationalisation of the African Peace and Security Architecture in the Sahelo-Saharan

(ACIRC) in a bid to find an immediate and innovative approach to palliate to the shortcomings of the ASF and its Rapid Deployment Capacity within the APSA[85]. ACIRC was finally adopted by the 21st Ordinary Session of the Assembly of the Union held in Addis Ababa, in May 2013.

AFISMA did not have enough time to flex its muscle on the ground because the UN launched the MINUSMA on April 2013 and the re-hatting ceremony took place on 01 July 2013. AU did not sign away and launched the consequently established on November 2013, the AU Mission for Mali and the Sahel (MISAHEL) in the context of thorny relation with the UNSC[86].

IV.3. The UN Peacekeeping Mission in Mali: Complex Crossroads

The United Nations has always paid a specific attention to conflict prevention and stability in Western Africa. In fact, the organization established its first regional conflict prevention and peacebuilding bureau (UNOWA) in Dakar on January 2002 at the request of the then UNSC Secretary General Koffi Annan.

---

region at: http://www.peaceau.org/en/article/ministerial-meeting-on-the-enhancement-of-security-cooperation-and-the-operationalisation-of-the-african-peace-and-security-architecture-in-the-sahelo-sahran-region#sthash.K5sU4OXg.dpuf, accessed July 2014.

[85] For an assessment of ACIRC vis-à-vis the ASF and its RDC, see Kodjo Tchioffo article 'Establishment of an African Capacity for Immediate Response to Crises (ACIRC): Analysis of this new-fangled mechanism vis-à-vis the African Standby force (ASF) and its Rapid Deployment Capability (RDC) within the African Peace and Security Architecture (APSA)' at https://www.academia.edu/Documents/in/African_Union_International_Peaceking, accessed July 2014.

[86] See the opening remarks by Dr Nkosazana Dlamini Zuma, Chairperson of the Commission of the African Union, at the 6th meeting of the support and follow-up group on the situation in Mali at http://www.peaceau.org/en/article/opening-remarks-by-h-e-dr-nkosazana-dlamini-zuma-chairperson-of-the-commission-of-the-african-union-1#sthash.YwRctXT2.dpuf, accessed July 2014.

UNOWA goal is to coordinate UN actions with regional bodies in West Africa with an emphasis on cross-border conflicts[87].

This part specifically assesses the United Nations role to sort out Mali crisis at its height with a specific consideration of issues pertaining to the path from AFISMA to MINUSMA, France influence in the UNSC notably through the positioning of Serval as a parallel force within MINUSMA and finally an appraisal of MINUSMA debuts in Mali.

IV.3.1. From AFISMA to MINUSMA: Challenging Period for ECOWAS/AU-UN Relationship

When Mali crisis started on January 2012, UNOWA chief, Said Djinnit visited Mali on 10 February to discuss the crisis with President ATT. On that occasion, UNOWA chief stressed the need for an immediate cessation of hostilities to allow an inclusive dialogue to be put in place. However, UNOWA main concerns were the transnational organized crime networks and the humanitarian consequences of the crisis[88]. These issues were reiterated by the UNSC in a press statement on 21 February 2012 calling for 'system-wide United Nations action to help combat the spread of illicit weapons and drug trafficking, piracy and terrorist activity in a cross-section of fragile countries already struggling to overcome the consequences of years of civil war and instability'[89].

---

[87] See 'UNOWA/ CNMC mandates' at http://unowa.unmissions.org/Default.aspx?tabid=871, accessed July 2014.
[88] See 'aid Djinnit visits Mali' at
http://unowa.unmissions.org/Default.aspx?tabid=765&ctl=Details&mid=1796&Itemid=2199 .
[89] See 'SC calls for system-wide UN action to combat Transnational Crime in West Africa' at
http://unowa.unmissions.org/Default.aspx?tabid=765&ctl=Details&mid=1796&Itemid=2217, accessed July 2014.

The minute ECOWAS took the lead to address the crisis, the UN sought to assist and advise the organization. Thus, UN representatives were present during most of ECOWAS meetings pertaining to Mali conflict. However, the UN position contrasted sharply with that of the ECOWAS. When the sub-regional body openly called for a military intervention, the UN was consistently reluctant to engage in such a path. So, it was no surprise that ECOWAS request for UN assistance to erect MICEMA were literally thrown in UN trash. For example on 5 July 2012, the UNSC resolution 2056 endorsed mediation efforts of ECOWAS and AU but 'postponed the consideration of an ECOWAS intervention force' (Freund, 2012). In diplomatic terms, the resolution put that the UNSC is ready to further examine the request once additional information had been provided regarding the objectives, means and modalities of the envisaged deployment and other possible measures[90]. More rude,

When the AU leadership crisis was unraveled in July 2012, the organization invigorated the Support and Follow-up Group on the Resolution of the Crises in Mali in order to garner vital international support. Thus, a draft Strategic Concept of the AFISMA was elaborated on 19 October 2012 during a tense meeting of the Support and Follow up group in Bamako boosted by the presence of the newly elected AUC Chairperson. The Strategic Concept of Operations (CONOPS) was submitted to the UNSC and the resolution 2085 was finally adopted on 20 December 2012, giving an international mandate to the African-led International Support Mission to Mali (AFISMA).

However, the resolution did not address vital issues related to the funding and the logistic support for AFISMA. Powerless, the AUC issued a press release the next day wishing that the UNSC allow rapid implementation of a logistic support package funded by statutory contributions from the UN budget, with the

---

[90] See the text of UNSC Resolution 2056 at
http://www.un.org/News/Press/docs/2012/sc10698.doc.htm, accessed July 2014.

view to facilitating the deployment and operations of the AFISMA[91]. The organization also called on 'African States and international partners to provide the necessary support, both financial and logistic, and in terms of training and equipment, to AFISMA and contribute generously to the Special Trust Fund set up for the benefit of Malian defense and security forces'[92].

So AFISMA was approved by the UNSC but remained an empty shell without partners funding and logistical support. This state of affairs was professed days earlier, on 16 December 2012 by US representative to the UNSC, Ambassador Susan Rice, which described AFISMA intervention plan as 'crap'. So, the UNSC allocated a paralytic mission to AU and ECOWAS that could not operate without massive international assistance.

When France launched Opération Serval, AU and ECOWAS felt a bitter-sweet taste. While they complimented France, they felt that it should have been AFISMA to take the lead in Mali in a bid to give weight to APSA slogan, African solutions to African Problems. This prompted African nations to promptly deploy troops on the ground as a face-saving measure and an attempt to play at least a lesser role. In this sense, Nigeria, ECOWAS most powerful state was the first to send troops in Mali.

More, AFISMA did not receive the support package it requested from the UN and the mission was short-circuited two months later by a decision of the UNSC on 25 April 2013 establishing the MINUSMA to take over the African-led mission.

---

[91] See 'African Union welcomes the adoption by the Security Council of the United Nations of Resolution 2085 (2012) on Mali' at http://www.peaceau.org/en/article/african-union-welcomes-the-adoption-by-the-security-council-of-the-united-nations-of-resolution-2085-2012-on-mali#sthash.viz3AGVY.dpuf, accessed July 2014.
[92] Ibid.

Greatly frustrated by the UNSC decision, the AUPSC met the same day and reacted in a harsh communiqué which noted 'with concern that Africa was not appropriately consulted in the drafting and consultation process that led to the adoption of the UN Security Council resolution authorizing' the MINUSMA to take over AFISMA[93]. Further, the AUPSC criticized bluntly the UNSC decision to establish MINUSMA stating that it completely ignored AU and ECOWAS mediation efforts which led to restoration of constitutional order and the adoption of a transitional roadmap and mobilization of the support of the international community through the Support and Follow-up Group on the situation in Mali[94]. But the AU finally complied with UNSC decision and MINUSMA took over AFISMA on 01 July 2014.

---

[93] See the Communiqué of the 371st PSC Meeting on the situation in Mali at
http://www.peaceau.org/en/article/communique-of-the-371st-psc-meeting-on-the-situation-in-mali#sthash.96dP9EV9.dpuf, accessed July 2014.
[94] Ibid.

Figure 5 - Head of AFISMA, Pierre Buyoya (center) sharing thoughts with the Head of MINUSMA, Bert Koenders (left) and UN Assistant Secretary-General for Peacekeeping Operations, Hervé Ladsous (right) during the re-hatting ceremony between AFISMA and MINUSMA; Copyright: Peace and Security Department of the African Union

Scholars argue that tensions between the AU and UN in Mali emanate respectively from 'diverging capabilities; risk-averse vs risk-assuming approaches to casualties; differing geopolitical calculations; and leadership rivalry' in the sphere of peace and security (Weiss and Welz, 2014).

The argumentation on leadership rivalry can be substantiated by a specific situation. The UN intends to develop a 'strategic framework to help the Sahel countries deal with the specific security, food, economic and social challenges faced by the region' (ICG, 2012, p7). On its side, the AU initiated the 'Nouakchott process' to coordinate efforts on the enhancement of security cooperation and the operationalization of the African Peace and Security Architecture (APSA) in the Sahelo-Saharan region. These initiatives focusing on Sahel include overlapping concerns but there is no evident coordination between the UN and the AU.

The idea of differing geopolitical calculations can be substantiated by few evidences. UNSG Ban Ki-moon appointment of Italian Romano Prodi as his Special Envoy for the Sahel on 09 October 2012 'disregarding competent candidates such as Mohammed Ibn Chambers, the former ECOWAS President' was another source of frustration for ECOWAS and the AU (Ibrahim, 2013). Furthermore, UNSG Ban Ki-moon later selected Dutch Bert Koenders on 17 May 2013 as his Special Representative and Head of MINUSMA to the detriment of the African choice, former President Pierre Buyoya. This also left a bitter taste in the AU.

While Weiss and Welz (2014) claim that Pierre Buyoya was discredited because of his background as coup leader in Burundi, Bert Koenders role as the head of ONUCI during Cote d'Ivoire crisis of 2011 has been perceived as controversial in Africa. Moreover, Bergamaschi (2013) suggests that Bert candidature was backed by France. This sounds like a reward for its smooth collaboration with France during 2011 crisis in Cote d'Ivoire.

Another point of contention at the level of geopolitical calculations was the allocation of a support package for AFISMA. While the AU pushed for the formulation of a support package funded by statutory contributions from the UN budget in a system similar to AMISOM funding, the UNSC adopted the 'non-committal formula of "voluntary or bilateral contributions" in running the force' (Ibrahim, 2013). AU formula has proven effective in AMISOM and this operation has become the torchbearer of APSA potential to thrive. In addition, Mali crisis has been analyzed by scholars to be similar to Somalia[95] prompting

---

[95] For an analogous comparison between Somalia and Mali, see Bloomberg article 'To Stabilize Mali, Look to Somalia's Lessons' at www.bloombergview.com/articles/2013-05-12/to-stabilize-mali-look-

Nicholson (2013) to ask: 'Can ECOWAS replicate the success of AMISOM in Mali?' But other quickly shows reserve and warns of the 'weakness of analogical thinking' (Thurston, 2013)[96].

At the level of capabilities and risk-taking, it can be said that UN Peacekeeping operation, while endowed, are risk-averse and often limit their actions to assist peace process in the context of cease fire agreement, even when their mandate is clearly based on robust chapter 7 operations. This is particularly visible in Africa where MONUSCO with its Force Intervention Brigade is often criticized as 'defining peacekeeping downward' (Hatcher and Perry, 2012). On its side, the AU insufficient capabilities, especially at the level of logistics and Communications and Information System (C3IS) has hinder the organization to match its discourse with action but the organization has proven to be highly risk-assuming notably in its mission in Somalia where it has been able to sustain high casualties.

It is important to assess UNSC geopolitical calculations on Mali, in a forum where France, a P5 member with vested interests in the region has been as the forefront of UN engagement in the country during the crisis of 2012 and 2013.

IV.3.2. France Lobby at work in the UNSC: Crafting the 'Parallel' Force within MINUSMA

It is well known that France is the most active permanent member of the UNSC P5 in Mali due to colonial past and sustained ties with the country. France has

---

to-somalia-s-lessons and Nicholson piece 'Can ECOWAS replicate the success of AMISOM in Mali?' at http://smallwarsjournal.com/blog/can-ecowas-replicate-the-success-of-amisom-in-mali, accessed July 2014.

[96] See also Mrkvicka article 'Intervention in Somalia: A Misguided Model for Success in Mali' at http://georgetownsecuritystudiesreview.org/2013/12/19/intervention-in-somalia-a-misguided-model-for-success-in-mali/, accessed July 2014.

been involved to secure international legitimacy for African efforts since the onset of the crisis. The country has been at the forefront to position Mali at the top of UNSC agenda during 2012. France drafted and circulated all the resolutions on Mali during 2012 and acted as a support for ECOWAS and AU endeavours.

Yet, the launch of Serval, while endorsed by all key players, revealed that France has planned its 'maskirovka' long in advance. In addition, France drafted the resolution 2100 of 25 April 2013 that authorized the transformation of AFISMA into MINUSMA and greatly upset AU and ECOWAS.

It is important to examine France motivations to input a resolution that put off African partners it previously supported. Officially, French Foreign Minister Laurent Fabius said to PressTV on 06 February 2013 that it is an advantage to shift AFISMA under UN umbrella because of financial resources that can leverage the global organization[97]. But, this argument is challenged by the fact that AFISMA was under UNSC mandate yet the UN did not want to allocate sufficient funds for the mission to be sustainable like AMISOM. So it appears that the UNSC did not finance AFISMA and pushed for MINUSMA under France guidance. Weiss and Welz (2014, p 897) of Chatham House enlighten that 'it was the UN secretariat (and France) that had exerted pressure, taking into account among other things the fact that several UN operations were about to close and qualified staff were available'.

Moreover, an in-depth scrutiny shows that France budget for OPEX has been stretched for more than 50 million Euros in three weeks after the start of

---

[97] See PressTV article 'France wants UN peacekeepers replace AFISMA in Mali' at www.presstv.com/detail/2013/02/07/287729/france-seeks-force-replacement-in-mali/, accessed July 2014.

Operation Serval[98]. This was unsustainable for a country facing a severe economic crisis.

Hitherto, on 26 March 2013, UNSCG Ban Ki-moon suggested to the UNSC that MINUSMA could be effective alongside a "parallel" counter-terrorism force that would 'operate under robust rules of engagement' and battle radical Islamists[99]. Albeit, French officials repeatedly argued that France intervened simply for a short-duration mission that will move off once the MINUSMA deploys[100], they perceived an opportunity in Ban's report and started to situate that Serval must play the role of the 'parallel' counter-terrorism force within the framework of MINUSMA[101].

Even if the P5 'had concerns as to how to define the relationship of the French forces and MINUSMA'[102], France manoeuvre was rewarded by the resolution 2100 establishing the MINUSMA. The document devoted a paragraph to legitimate France military presence in Northern Mali within the framework of MINUSMA. The resolution specifically authorized France to use 'all necessary

[98] See Le Monde article 'Mali : l'opération Serval a coûté "autour de 50 millions d'euros" en trois semaines'at www.lemonde.fr/afrique/article/2013/01/31/mali-l-operation-serval-a-coute-autour-de-50-millions-d-euros-en-trois-semaines_1825509_3212.html, accessed July 2014.
[99] See the Report of the Secretary-General on the situation in Mali at http://www.un.org/en/ga/search/view_doc.asp?symbol=S/2013/189, accessed July 2014.
[100] For example Xinhua reported on 06 February 2013 France President affirming that the country's troops will return home when the UN will take the lead. See the article 'French forces not to stay in Mali for long: defense minister' at http:// english.peopledaily.com.cn/90777/8123647.html.
[101] See for example France24 article 'Mali needs more than 11,000 peacekeepers, UN says' which puts that Ban Ki-moon suggestion is a 'clear signal that France will have to maintain a strong military involvement in the conflict' at www.france24.com/en/20130327-ban-ki-moon-says-11200-troops-needed-mali-un-peacekeeping/ .
[102] See the think-thank Security Council Report article 'Resolution Establishing a UN Mission in Mali' that give specific insights on the discussions before the adoption of the resolution at http://www.whatsinblue.org/2013/04/resolution-establishing-a-un-mission-in-mali.php .

means [...] to intervene in support of elements of MINUSMA when under imminent and serious threat'[103].

France mandate has been renewed by the resolution 2164 of the UNSC in the framework of MINUSMA on 25 June 2014. Operation Serval was also transformed to Operation Barkhane on 01 August 2014 to overview terrorists' threats within the Sahel. For Bombande and Van Tuijl (2014), the regionalisation of France operation adds confusion and ambiguity 'in terms of policy imperatives, command, control, and accountability' for the UNSC regarding France endeavours.

France influence within MINUSMA went beyond securing an international mandate that legitimate the long-term presence for its troops. Also, for the first time the country was granted five OTC contracts for its companies to build MINUSMA infrastructure in northern Mali for a value of 34.7 million Euros[104]. For Agence Ecofin (2013) these contracts simply rewarded France for operation Serval which stopped the move of rebel groups southward[105]. In any case, France was able to craft a long-term strategic position within MINUSMA.

Considering all these insights, it is important to assess MINUSMA debuts in Mali especially the coordination between MINUSMA and France 'parallel' force. Also, the perception of MINUSMA role at the local level should be investigated as well as the attitude of regional players towards the mission.

---

[103] See the text of resolution 2100 establishing MINUSMA at
http://www.un.org/en/peacekeeping/missions/minusma/documents/mali%20_2100_E_.pdf .
[104] See France Foreign Ministry website article 'Mali - Attribution de contrats à des entreprises françaises au profit de la MINUSMA (13 mars 2014)' at www.diplomatie.gouv.fr/fr/dossiers-pays/mali/la-france-et-le-mali/evenements-19439/article/mali-attribution-de-contrats-a-des .
[105] See Agence Ecofin article 'L'ONU récompense la France au Mali en attribuant des marchés à ses entreprises' at www.agenceecofin.com/gestion-publique/1303-18356-l-onu-recompense-la-france-au-mali-en-attribuant-des-marches-a-ses-entreprises .

IV.3.3. MINUSMA Débuts in Mali: Appraisal of the Operation Outset

According to Leibow (2013), MINUSMA is 'poised for failure' because 'there is no peace to keep' despite the littering of the rebellion by Serval and AFISMA. She adds that the UN operation was deployed in an environment that did not fulfill UN key principles of peacekeeping specifically the consent of parties, impartiality and the non-use of force except in self-defence and defence of the mandate (Leibow, 2013).

However, Bergamaschi (2013) suggests that MINUSMA 'played a role' in the smooth conduct of presidential elections of 2013 which has seen the victory of Ibrahim Boubakar Keita (IBK). She also submits that a maiden challenge for MINUSMA has been the 'conversion of the 6,000 AFISMA troops into blue helmets' (Bergamaschi, 2013, p 1). On this sense, she argues that Burkina Faso troop's contribution was below the minimum requirement of the UN and that Chad contingent has been involved in human rights violations (Bergamaschi, 2013).

Furthermore, Bergamaschi (2013) draws attention to MINUSMA defies on issues of leadership, coordination and capacity. In this vein, she sets forth that the 'leadership and the division of labour within MINUSMA have been contested' with France backing Bert Koenders to the detriment of Pierre Buyoya for the post of SRSG and Rwanda Major-General Jean-Bosco Kazura appointed force commander of the MINUSMA in spite of Major-General Shehu Adbulkadir of Nigeria or Chad Major-General Oumar Bikimo.

For the Support Committee of Chadian Armed Forces in Mali (Fatim), Chad has been 'betrayed' by the UN which displays a 'notorious lack of recognition' of

Chad achievements to help secure northern Mali[106]. This appears to have accelerated the withdrawal of Chad troops which had already started on April 2013.

Nigeria reaction was very tough as the country completely pulled out of MINUSMA on 18 July 2013 during a summit of ECOWAS in Abuja. The official justification that Nigeria move was motivated by internal struggle notably Boko Haram threat offset the argument that Nigeria, the regional superpower felt humiliated by the sidelining of its candidate in favour of Rwanda. For Kane (2013) Nigeria was 'torn between international glory and domestic security'.

Still at the level of leadership and coordination, Bergamaschi (2013) notes that 'the commander of the French forces, General Vianney Pillet, appears to be the real chief of military operations in practice, in collaboration with Operation Serval commanders'. This observation raises the issue of the quality of command and control within MINUSMA and outputs the real level of France clout within the mission.

Further, Bergamaschi (2013) adds that MINUSMA is 'painfully short of resources' especially logistical assets. It is attention-grabbing to remind that one of the reasons AFISMA was dismantled was the lack of financial and logistical resources. Yet, MINUSMA finds itself in the same situation. So, it is justified to inquire if the replacement of AFISMA by MINUSMA was indispensable.

Later, Bergamaschi (2013) joins Lebow (2013) and Gowan (2013) in the line of thinking that MINUSMA was established on a fragile basis for intervention. Precisely, she argues that in the presence of a weak Ouagadougou preliminary

---

[106] See 'Mise en place du commandement militaire de la Minusma. Le Tchad a-t-il été trahi ?' at http://abidjandirect.net/index2.php?page=poli&id=8237 .

peace agreement between Bamako and the MNLA, 'MINUSMA is a potentially flawed peace operation'. (Bergamaschi, 2013).

At the local level, MINUSMA attracts mostly jobless Malians expecting to find well-remunerated position in the mission. But, Mali public opinion specifically the Online Newspaper MaliActu has not been soft with MINUSMA labelling it 'AMUSEMENT' meaning a big joke in French[107]. For this newspaper, MINUSMA troops are more preoccupied by a luxurious and carnal lifestyle in Bamako than fulfilling its mandate under resolution 2100 in the northern part of the country[108]. Further, the newspaper suggests that recent inflation in Mali that affects locals is a direct result of massive presence of MINUSMA and other international institutions in the country. In another article, it is suggested that MINUSMA feels 'insecure' in Mali as its troops become 'invisible' whenever they is a need to maintain a sufficient level of security for the locals or the government[109].

For Bombande and Van Tuijl (2014), MINUSMA 'has not succeeded in breaking down its mandate in simple terms for the people of Mali' and therefore its mandate must be reframed to 'incorporate human security principles [...] and outreach strategy that will clarify what it intends to deliver' for Malians. Oumar Mariko, an influent Malian political leader has set forth that France and MINUSMA are abettors of the MNLA after attacks on Mali prime minister during his visit of Kidal on 17 May 2013.

In all, a UNSG report on the situation in Mali submitted on 09 June 2014 is a blatant recognition of MINUSMA limits since its inception. UNSG Ban Ki-

---

[107] 'See Mali Actu article 'Minusma ou Amusement ?' at http://maliactu.net/minusma-ou-amusement/ .

[108] Ibid.

[109] See MaliActu article 'MINUSMA : L'insécurité d'une mission de Sécurité' at http://maliactu.net/minusma-linsecurite-dune-mission-de-securite/ .

moon acknowledges that 'after initial improvements in 2013, the security situation in northern Mali has deteriorated since the beginning of 2014' despite the presence of MINUSMA troops and the existence of France 'parallel' peace enforcement force.

Chap V. Conclusions and Future Research

The study validates the proposition that the Malian turmoil is a complex mixture of cumulated historic grievances, poor governance and failure of international aid, whose aftershock continued into 2012-2013. The conflict resolution mechanisms entail bilateral and multilateral arrangements operating in a post-colonial and post-cold war framework. These peacekeeping arrangements evolve in a cooperation/competition logic embedded in power-play strategies haunted by the fantasy of burden sharing.

This book raison d'être stemmed from the observation that Mali was still suffering aftershocks of its protracted crises which climaxed on 2012 and 2013. The research sought to critically dissects the multiple and self-reinforcing dimensions of Mali crises and methodically untie the intertwined bilateral, regional and global arrangements established in order to secure a lasting peace and restore Mali authority over its entire territory.

To channel the analysis, Mali crises were investigated in the lenses of a post-colonial and post-cold war francophone African nation-state challenged by translocal terrorism and transnational organized crime tangled amid socio-economic as well as ethno-religious tensions in the dialectic of creed, greed and grievance theory.

The research exposed that during 2012 and 2013, Mali faced its fourth Touareg crisis which evolved into a secessionist rebellion later embedded with local Islamist terrorists' movements. The dimension captured was the shift from a grievance-driven upheaval to a nationalist secessionist uprising and the dynamics of amalgamation/differentiation of the Touareg movement with translocal terrorists' groups nurtured by creed and greed.

A critical facet unraveled by the research is the abysmal political and constitutional crisis facing Mali during 2012 and 2013 stemming from power-play interactions between old political class and new political elites entwined with military rivalries in the backyard of a coup d'état. The study substantiates that the political and constitutional crisis stem from a post-colonial 'belly' and 'phallus' democratic system. It is also exposed that Mali democracy of façade is particularly tolerated by and enmeshed with international donor strategic complacency. Mali is a donor-darling where both the ruling elites and the country's donors turn a blind eye to encysted corruption and management flaws in a self-preserving system correlating with Moyo's 'dead aid'.

A key feature of the political and constitutional crisis is its spatial dimension, concentrated to the capital Bamako and its surroundings exclusively in the south of Mali. Unwittingly, it crafts a self-reinforcing effect with the secessionist and terrorist crisis in northern Mali where rebels can control large parts of territory without facing significant resistance.

Yet, Mali 'special ties' with France, its former colonial power as well as the country's membership in sub-regional, continental and global arrangements precisely the 'core countries', ECOWAS, AU and the UN served as an instrument to put in place specific initiatives to assist the country restore peace and secure its authority over its territory.

International intervention in Mali was structured around three decisive stakes specifically the establishment of viable transitional institutions, the mediation with Touareg-led rebels and later peacekeeping missions to deny a safe haven to terrorists in the context of burden-sharing as an emerging principle.

While ECOWAS was able to secure a swift establishment of transitional institutions ten days after the coup, its mediation has been flawed on many grounds. The book notably pinpoints the leadership struggle for the mediation supervision between ECOWAS and the AU within the APSA framework and later the mess with the choice of President Compaoré of Burkina-Faso as ECOWAS mediator in Mali considering the history of short war between the countries over Agacher strip. These intrinsic weaknesses of the mediation are later aggravated by undue influence on the transition by ECOWAS mediators seeking inter-alia to position their henchmen at key positions in Mali transitional government.

Another point of contention is Algeria and Mauritania, key members with Mali of the 'pays du champ' or 'core' countries initiative which aimed to coordinate these states efforts to address cross-border terrorism and transnational organized crimes. The research demonstrates that the 'core' countries were skeptical about ECOWAS mediation and appeared locked in a rigid logic of non-intervention that hindered the efficiency of decisions taken at regional level.

In parallel to the mediation efforts, ECOWAS and later the AU sought to use force in order to rout out Islamist terrorists from Northern Mali. The research shows that ECOWAS and AU 'va-t-en guerre' rhetoric particularly the establishment of MICEMA and AFISMA did not match the resources at the disposal of these organizations whether financial or vital logistical assets. In addition, the study exposes that the political determination of these organizations within the APSA was hindered by the lack of support from the UN despite the emerging burden-sharing principle.

Further, the study shows that AU and UN relationship during Mali crisis has been a milieu of contentions and frustrations especially for the AU. The study examines carefully the geopolitical principles of the AU and the UN in Mali in the lenses of Weiss and Welz (2014) theory of 'diverging capabilities; risk-averse vs risk-assuming approaches to casualties; differing geopolitical calculations; and leadership rivalry'. The study opens that notwithstanding the overall discourse of burden-sharing, the AU and the UN means and overall approach on peacekeeping are neither consistent nor harmonized as reflected by the rasping transition from AFISMA to MINUSMA.

The study also reflects on France strategy during the crisis notably its official lip service and façade backing of ECOWAS and AU peacekeeping initiatives while it was preparing its own operation in the context of a 'maskrivoka'. Despite Milne (2013) argument that Mali crisis was a spillover resulting from NATO military intervention in Libya on 2011, the research has proven that France operation Serval has been largely acclaimed and Delaporte (2013) even draw lessons for future international operations with the watchwords 'Fight Alone, Supply Together' to capture France air refueling by the USA.

The book further assesses France lobby at work in the UNSC during the establishment of MINUSMA particularly the crafting of a 'parrallel' force within the UN operation. The research shows that France has been able to orient UNSC decisions and resolutions in the sense of its interests especially securing a long-term presence in Mali and the region in the framework of the UN. While some can put that France has also signed a bilateral military agreement with Mali so it can live without the UN legal framework, it is crucial to argue like Ecclesiastes (4:9-12) that 'two are better than one, because they have a good

116

return for their labor'. This is for instance visible with the five contracts secured by France for its companies to build MINUSMA infrastructure.

The research finally appraises MINUSMA debuts in Mali in the context of African frustrations and France influence within the operation. The research corroborates UNSCG Ban Ki-moon report of 09 June 2014 that the situation in Northern Mali has worsened since the establishment of MINUSMA. So, in the current state of affairs, MINUSMA is impotent and despite the support of France 'parallel' force, the peacekeeping mission has been unable to maintain Mali authority over its northern provinces as attested by the events of 17 May 2014 in Kidal.

Further research can investigate comparatively Mali and Central African Republic conflicts in an attempt to consolidate this new pattern of tangled peacekeeping in post-cold war and post-colonial francophone Africa where the UN intervene to replace an African peacekeeping operation while France still plays the gendarme in its former colonies.

Bibliography/ References

Adeniji, O. (1997). Mechanisms for Conflict Management in West Africa: Politics of Harmonization. *The Journal of Humanitarian Assistance.*

AFP. (2012, February 07). *Tuareg rebels not bound by truce talks.* Retrieved June 06, 2014, from AFP: http://www.news24.com/Africa/News/Tuareg-rebels-not-bound-by-truce-talks-20120207

Afrik.com. (2012, February 06). *Mali : le MNLA refuse l'appel au cessez-le-feu proposé par Alger.* Retrieved June 09, 2014, from Afrik.com: http://www.afrik.com/breve38947.html

Agence Ecofin. (2014, March 13). *L'ONU récompense la France au Mali en attribuant des marchés à ses entreprises.* Retrieved July 07, 2014, from Ecofin:

http://www.agenceecofin.com/gestion-publique/1303-18356-l-onu-recompense-la-france-au-mali-en-attribuant-des-marches-a-ses-entreprises

AJCS. (2013). *French Intervention in Mali: Causes and Consequences.* Al Jazeera Center for Studies.

Alvarado, D. (2012). INDEPENDENT AZAWAD: Tuaregs, Jihadists, and an Uncertain Future for Mali. *notes internacionals CIDOB- Barcelona Centre for International Affairs ISSN: 201.*

Anderson, B. (2006). *Imagined Communities: Reflections on the Origin and Spread of Nationalism.* Verso.

Arieff, A. (2012). *Algeria and the Crisis in Mali.* Actuelles de l'Ifri.

Arieff, A. (2013). *Crisis in Mali* . Congressional Research Service.

Assadeck, A. (2012, April 12). *Le deal France – MNLA.* Retrieved June 22, 2014, from Tamtaminfo: http://www.tamtaminfo.com/le-deal-france-mnla/

Attakpah, S. A. (2012, July 16). *The Mali Crisis – A reminder that ECOWAS' Early Warning System is grossly inadequate.* Retrieved June 08, 2014, from Afro Euro: http://afroeuro.org/magazine/?p=5813

AU. (2004). *MoU in the Area of Peace and Security between the AU and the RECs.* African Union.

AU. (2012). *African Union welcomes the adoption by the Security Council of the United Nations of Resolution 2085 (2012) on Mali* . African Union.

AU. (2012). *African Union welcomes the adoption by the Security Council of the United Nations of Resolution 2085 (2012) on Mali* . African Union Commission.

AU. (2012). *Report of the Peace and Security Council on its Activities and the State of Peace and Security in Africa* . African Union.

AU. (2012). *The African Union concerned by the situation in the Sahel Ministerial meeting of the AU Peace and Security Council in Bamako.* African Union.

AU. (2012). *The African Union strongly condemns the action of the mutineers who announced that they have taken power in Mali* . African Union.

AU. (2013). *Communiqué of the 371st PSC Meeting on the situation in Mali.* African Union.

Badibanga, S. (2013, January 04). *Mali : « Ansar Dine essaye de retarder l'intervention militaire ».* Retrieved June 07, 2014, from Afrik.com: http://www.afrik.com/mali-ansar-dine-essaye-de-retarder-l-intervention-militaire

Barluet, A. (2012, March 23). *Paris tourne sans regrets la page du «mauvais élève» ATT.* Retrieved June 08, 2014, from Le Figaro: http://www.lefigaro.fr/international/2012/03/22/01003-20120322ARTFIG00755-paris-tourne-sans-regrets-la-page-du-mauvais-eleve-att.php

Batou, J. (2013). *Mali: A Neo-Colonial Operation Disguised as an Anti-Terrorist Intervention.* Retrieved March 14, 2014, from New Politics: http://newpol.org/content/mali-neo-colonial-operation-disguised-anti-terrorist-intervention

Bayart, J.-F., Ellis, S., & Hibou, B. (2000). The Criminalization of the State in Africa. *Canadian Journal of African Studies / Revue Canadienne des Études Africaines,* 454-456.

BBC. (2013, August 22). *Belmokhtar's militants 'merge' with Mali's Mujao.* Retrieved March 12, 2014, from bbc.com: http://www.bbc.com/news/world-us-canada-23796920

BBC Afrique. (2012, November 13). *La France n'interviendra pas au Mali.* Retrieved June 02, 2014, from BBC Afrique: http://www.bbc.co.uk/afrique/region/2012/11/121113_mali_france_defense_minister.shtml

Bergamaschi, I. (2013, August 15). *Collapsed, failed, criminalized? Notes on the State in Mali – By Isaline Bergamaschi.* Retrieved March 13, 2014, from African Arguments: http://africanarguments.org/2013/08/15/collapsed-failed-criminalized-notes-on-the-state-in-mali-by-isaline-bergamaschi/

Bergamaschi, I. (2013). *French Military Intervention in Mali: Inevitable, Consensual yet Insufficient.* Retrieved March 13, 2014, from International Journal of Stability, Security and Development: http://www.stabilityjournal.org/article/view/sta.bb/70

Bergamaschi, I. (2013, April 01). *Mali: how to avoid making the same mistakes.* Retrieved March 13, 2014, from Good Governance Africa: http://gga.org/stories/editions/aif-10-aid-the-bottomless-pit/mali-how-to-avoid-making-the-same-mistakes

Bergamaschi, I. (2013, September 16). *MINUSMA: first steps, achievements and challenges.* Retrieved March 13, 2014, from Norwegian Peacebuilding Resource Centre: http://www.peacebuilding.no/var/ezflow_site/storage/original/application/89da563832be4b62d09bc99edc0cf080.pdf

Bergamaschi, I. (2013). *MINUSMA: initial steps, achievements.* Norwegian Peacebuilding Resource Centre (NOREF).

Bergamaschi, I. (2013). *The fall of a donor darling: the role of aid in Mali's crisis.* Retrieved March 13, 2014, from academia.edu: https://www.academia.edu/5352297/The_Fall_of_a_Donor_Darling_The_Role_of_Aid_in_Malis_Crisis

Bergamaschi, I. (2013). *The French Military Intervention in Mali: Not Exactly Françafrique, But Definitely Post-colonial.* Retrieved March 14, 2014, from academia.edu: https://www.academia.edu/5328698/The_French_Military_Intervention_in_Mali_Not_Exactly_Francafrique_But_Definitely_Post-colonial

Bergamaschi, I. (2013, March 31). *The role of governance and aid in Mali's crisis.* Retrieved March 14, 2014, from ALJAZEERA: http://www.aljazeera.com/indepth/opinion/2013/03/201331412468880930.html

Blanquer, J.-M. (2013, January 15). *France: We're not the pacifists you think we are.* Retrieved June 08, 2013, from CNN: http://www.cnn.com/2013/01/15/opinion/france-mali-opinion-blanquer/

Boisbouvier, C. (2010, February 10). *50 years later, Françafrique is alive and well.* Retrieved June 04, 2014, from RFI: http://www.english.rfi.fr/africa/20100216-50-years-later-francafrique-alive-and-well

Boisbouvier, C. (2012, April 02). *Ibrahim Ag Mohamed Assaleh: «Le MNLA négociera avec des autorités légitimes».* Retrieved June 05, 2014, from RFI: http://www.rfi.fr/afrique/20120402-ibrahim-ag-mohamed-assaleh-Mali-Azawad-Tombouctou-Kidal-Gao-rebellion/

Boitiaux, C. (2012, October 02). *Nord-Mali : Alger négocie secrètement avec les islamistes d'Ansar Dine.* Retrieved July 08, 2014, from AFP/France 24: http://www.france24.com/fr/20121002-nord-mali-algerie-negocier-islamistes-ansar-dine-touareg/

Boitiaux, C. (2013, January 19). *Le double jeu d'Alger face à la crise au Sahel.* Retrieved July 07, 2014, from AFP/France 24: http://www.france24.com/fr/20130119-algerie-double-jeu-strategie-crise-sahel-mali/

Bombande, E., & Tuijl, P. V. (2014, June 24). *Can MINUSMA's Mandate Include the People of Mali?* Retrieved July 07, 2014, from The International Peace Institute (IPI): http://theglobalobservatory.org/analysis/770-minusma-mandate-include-people-mali.html

Boutellis, A., & Williams, P. D. (2013, May 15). *Disagreements Over Mali Could Sour More Than the Upcoming African Union Celebration.* Retrieved March 14, 2014, from Global Observatory: http://theglobalobservatory.org/analysis/502-disagreements-over-mali-could-sour-more-than-the-upcoming-african-union-celebration.html

Callimachi, R. (2013, February 14). *In Timbuktu, Al-Qaida Left Behind A Manifesto.* Retrieved June 09, 2014, from AP: http://bigstory.ap.org/article/timbuktu-al-qaida-left-behind-strategic-plans

Callimachi, R. (2013, February 04). *People of Timbuktu Save Manuscripts from Invaders.* Retrieved June 09, 2014, from AP: http://bigstory.ap.org/article/people-timbuktu-save-manuscripts-invaders

Campbell, J. (2013, March 15). *How to Stabilize Northern Mali.* Retrieved March 23, 2014, from Council on Foreign Relations: http://blogs.cfr.org/campbell/2013/03/15/how-to-stabilize-northern-mali/

Carayol, R. (2013, February 02). *"Papa Hollande" au Mali.* Retrieved March 18, 2014, from Jeune Afrique: http://www.jeuneafrique.com/Article/ARTJAWEB20130202235649/

Carayol, R. (2013, August 14). *Au Nord-Mali, les groupes armés touaregs et arabes font un pas vers l'unité.* Retrieved April 17, 2014, from Jeune Afrique: http://www.jeuneafrique.com/Article/ARTJAWEB20130814145116/

Carayol, R. (2013, December 25). *Intégrisme : OPA sur le Sahel*. Retrieved March 18, 2014, from Jeune Afrique: http://www.jeuneafrique.com/Articles/Dossier/JA2762p026.xml0/tchad-senegal-maroc-nigerintegrisme-opa-sur-le-sahel.html

Carayol, R. (2013, April 16). *Mali : à Kidal, tout reste à faire*. Retrieved April 16, 2014, from Jeune Afrique: http://www.jeuneafrique.com/Article/JA2726p034.xml0/

Carayol, R. (2013, 06 04). *Mali : alliances touarègues et sables mouvants*. Retrieved March 16, 2014, from Jeune Afrique: http://www.jeuneafrique.com/Article/JA2733p034.xml0/

Carayol, R. (2013, 09 09). *Mali : jihadistes sur le retour*. Retrieved March 18, 2014, from Jeune Afrique: http://www.jeuneafrique.com/Article/JA2747p038.xml0/

Charbonneau, B., & Chafer, T. (2014). *Peace Operations in the Francophone World: Global Governance Meets Post-Colonialism*. Routledge.

Chrisafis, A. (2013, January 13). *Mali: high stakes in 'Hollande's war'*. Retrieved June 09, 2014, from The Guardian: http://www.theguardian.com/world/2013/jan/13/mali-high-stakes-francois-hollande

Christakis, T., & Bannelier, K. (2013, January 24). *French Military Intervention in Mali: It's Legal but... Why? Part I*. Retrieved March 14, 2014, from Ejil: Talk!: http://www.ejiltalk.org/french-military-intervention-in-mali-its-legal-but-why-part-i/

Collier, P., & Hoeffler, A. (2000). *Greed and Grievance in Civil War*. The World Bank Policy Research Working Papers.

Coulibaly, F. (2012, October 19). *Marche de protestation contre la CEDEAO : La COPAM considère que toute intervention étrangère au Mali ne fera que repousser à plus loin la libération du nord*. Retrieved June 02, 2014, from Maliweb/L'Independant: http://www.maliweb.net/politique/marche-de-protestation-contre-la-cedeao-la-copam-considere-que-toute-intervention-etrangere-au-mali-ne-fera-que-repousser-a-plus-loin-la-liberation-du-nord-100347.html

Crumley, B. (2010, July 09). *Ambassador Blasts France's Relations with its African Allies*. Retrieved May 22, 2014, from Time: http://content.time.com/time/world/article/0,8599,2002788,00.html

Dao, B. (2013, April 18). *Occupation de la ville de Kidal par le MNLA : Les autorités de la transition doivent s'expliquer au peuple*. Retrieved June 21, 2014, from Slate Afrique: http://www.slateafrique.com/169289/occupation-de-la-ville-de-kidal-par-le-mnla-les-autorites-de-la-transition-doivent-s%E2%80%99explique

Daou, O. (2011, November 25). *Coopération Union européenne et le Mali : Plus de 32 milliards pour la sécurité au Nord Mali*. Retrieved June 08, 2014, from Maliweb/L'Indicateur du Renouveau: http://www.maliweb.net/economie/cooperation/coopration-union-europenne-et-le-mali-plus-de-32-milliards-pour-la-scurit-au-nord-mali-36205.html

Delaporte, M. (2013, June 17). *French Lessons From Mali: Fight Alone, Supply Together.* Retrieved June 22, 2014, from Breaking Defense: http://breakingdefense.com/2013/06/french-lessons-from-mali-fight-alone-supply-together/

Derrida, J. (1983). *Dissemination .* University of Chicago Press.

Diallo, G. (2004). Mauritania – Neither Arab nor African. *Nordiska Afrikainstitutet.*

DIOP, M. D. (2012, April 02). *Tombouctou sous la menace de la Charia.* Retrieved May 08, 2014, from JournalduMali.com: http://www.journaldumali.com/article.php?aid=4447

Dockins, P. (2013, March 28). *Former US Ambassador: Algeria Key to Stabilizing Mali.* Retrieved July 03, 2014, from VOA: http://www.voanews.com/content/former-us-ambassador-algeria-key-to-stabilizing-mali/1630635.html

Douhet, M. d. (2012, February 10). *Mali: le spectre de la division touarègue.* Retrieved June 06, 2014, from Groupe Express-Roularta: http://www.lexpress.fr/actualite/monde/afrique/mali-le-spectre-de-la-division-touaregue_1080898.html;Mozilla/5.0

ECOWAS. (1999). *Protocol Relating to the Mechanism For Conflict Prevention, Management, Resolution, Peace-Keeping And Security.* Economic Community of West African States.

ECOWAS. (2012). *Emergency Mini-Summit Of Ecowas Heads Of State And Government On The Situation In Mali.* Economic Community of West African States Commission.

Elbinawi, H. (2013, January 28). *Nigeria Serving Imperialism In Mali.* Retrieved June 23, 2014, from Sahara Reporters: http://saharareporters.com/2013/01/28/nigeria-serving-imperialism-mali-harun-elbinawi

Elischer, S. (2013, February 12). *After Mali Comes Niger : West Africa's Problems Migrate East.* Retrieved June 23, 2014, from Foreign Affairs: http://www.foreignaffairs.com/articles/138931/sebastian-elischer/after-mali-comes-niger

Enge, U., & Porto, J. G. (2010). *Towards an African Peace and Security Regime.* Ashgate .

Engel, U., & Nugent, P. (2009). *Respacing Africa.* Leiden: Brill Academic Publishers.

Engel, U., & Olsen, G. R. (2010). Authority, sovereignty and Africa's changing regimes of territorialisation. *Working Paper Series Numero 7 of the Graduate Centre Humanities and Social Sciences of Leipzig University.*

Fairclough, N. (2001). The Dialectics of Discourse. *Textus ,* 3-10.

Fairclough, N. (2010). *Critical Discourse Analysis - The Critical Study of Language.* Longman.

Felix, B., & Irish, J. (2013, January 12). *France bombs Mali rebels, African states ready troops.* Retrieved June 06, 2014, from Reuters: http://www.sott.net/article/256219-France-bombs-Mali-rebels-African-states-ready-troops

Foucault, M. (1972). *The Archaeology of Knowledge.* Routledge.

Francis, D. J. (2013). *The regional impact of the armed conflict and French intervention in Mali*. The Norwegian Peacebuilding Resource Centre (NOREF).

Gearan, A. (2012, October 29). *U.S. pushes Algeria to support military intervention in Mali.* Retrieved July 07, 2014, from Washington Post: http://www.washingtonpost.com/world/us-pushes-algeria-to-support-military-intervention-in-mali/2012/10/29/fee8df44-21a3-11e2-92f8-7f9c4daf276a_story.html

Gibbs, D. N. (2013, April 01). *Celebrating French Intervention in Mali*. Retrieved June 08, 2014, from Fairness & Accuracy In Reporting: http://fair.org/extra-online-articles/celebrating-french-intervention-in-mali/

Goïta, M. (2014, May 20). *French intervention, EU and UN. African solution for African problems?* Retrieved June 12, 2014, from Instituto Español de Estudios Estratégicos: http://www.ieee.es/Galerias/fichero/docs_opinion/2014/DIEEEO56-2014_SituacionMali_Prof.Mabadi_ENGLISH.pdf

Goodhand, J., Vaux, T., & Walker, R. (2002). *Conducting Conflict Assessments: Guidance Notes*. DFID.

Grasa, R., & Mateos, O. (2010). Conflict, Peace and Security in Africa: an Assessment and New Questions After 50 Years of African Independence. *Institut Català International*.

Guindo, A., & Tiékorobani. (2012, July 03). *Le président du MNLA évacué par l'armée burkinabè*. Retrieved June 22, 2014, from MaliWeb/ Proces Verbal: http://www.maliweb.net/insecurite/le-president-du-mnla-evacue-par-larmee-burkinabe-77160.html

Gurr, T. R. (1970). *Why Men Rebel*. Princeton University Press.

Hadzi-Vidanovic, V. (2013, January 23). *France Intervenes in Mali Invoking both SC Resolution 2085 and the Invitation of the Malian Government – Redundancy or Legal Necessity?* Retrieved June 08, 2014, from Ejil: Talk!: http://www.ejiltalk.org/france-intervenes-in-mali-invoking-both-sc-resolution-2085-and-the-invitation-of-the-malian-government-redundancy-or-legal-necessity/

Haidara, B. (2014, May 05). *Serval: prémisse d'une présence militaire française definitive au Mali*. Retrieved June 08, 2014, from terangaweb.com: http://terangaweb.com/serval-premisse-dune-presence-militaire-francaise-definitive-au-mali-1/

Hall, B. S. (2011). *A History of Race in Muslim West Africa (1600-1960)*. Cambridge University Press.

Hall, B., Lecocq, B., Mann, G., & Whitehouse, B. (2013, May 14). *Mali: Which way forward? A chat with Bruce Hall, Baz Lecocq, Gregory Mann and Bruce Whitehouse*. Retrieved March 13, 2014, from African Arguments: http://africanarguments.org/2013/05/14/mali-which-way-forward-a-chat-with-bruce-hall-baz-lecocq-gregory-mann-and-bruce-whitehouse/

Hamza, A. (2012, December 14). *Can France and Algeria find common ground on Mali?* Retrieved July 09, 2014, from France 24: http://www.france24.com/en/20121212-algeria-mali-france-common-ground-crisis-military-intervention/

Hansen, A. (2008, February 08). *The French Military in Africa.* Retrieved May 22, 2014, from Council on Foreign Relations: http://www.cfr.org/france/french-military-africa/p12578

Heath-Kellya, C., Jarvisb, L., & Baker-Beallc, C. (2013). Critical Terrorism Studies: Practice, Limits and Experience. *Critical Studies on Terrorism,* 1-10.

Helly, D., & Rocca, C. (2013). *The Mali crisis and Africa-Europe relations.* ECDPM.

Herbst, J. (2000). *States and Power in Africa: Comparative Lessons in Authority and Control (Princeton Studies in International History and Politics) .* Princeton University Press.

Hirsch, A. (2012, October 22). *France to send drones to Mali in fight against al-Qaida-backed insurgents.* Retrieved June 07, 2014, from heguardian.com: http://www.theguardian.com/world/2012/oct/22/france-drones-mali-insurgents

Huckabey, J. M. (2013). *Al Qaeda in Mali: The Defection Connections.* Orbis.

Huntington, S. P. (1993). The Clash of Civilizations? *Foreign Affairs.*

Huntington, S. P. (1996). *The Clash of Civilizations and the Remaking of World Order.* Reed Business Information, Inc.

Ibrahim, J. (2013, January 12). *The Malian Crisis: Time for ECOWAS Leadership.* Retrieved July 06, 2014, from Official Blog of the Centre for Democracy Development in West Africa: http://blog.cddwestafrica.org/2013/01/the-malian-crisis-time-for-ecowas-leadership/

ICG. (2013). *Mali: Security, Dialogue and Meaningful Reform.* International Crisis Group.

Irish, J., & Felix, B. (2013, January 11). *Malian army beats back Islamist rebels with French help.* Retrieved June 08, 2014, from Reuters: http://www.reuters.com/article/2013/01/11/us-mali-rebels-idUSBRE90912Q20130111

Jackson, R., Smyth, M. B., & Gunning, J. (2009). *Critical Terrorism Studies: A New Research Agenda.* Routledge.

Jackson, R., Smyth, M. B., & Gunning, J. (2009). *Critical Terrorism Studies: A New Research Agenda.* Routledge.

Jakobsen, T. G. (2012). *The Causes of Civil War.* Retrieved May 21, 2014, from Popular Social Science: http://www.popularsocialscience.com/2012/11/05/the-causes-of-civil-war/

Jauvert, V., & Halifa-Legrand, S. (2013, February 10). *Mali : histoire secrète d'une guerre surprise.* Retrieved June 07, 2014, from Le nouvel Observateur: http://globe.blogs.nouvelobs.com/archive/2013/02/08/mali-histoire-secrete-d-une-guerre-surprise.html

Jorio, R. D. (2013, June 10). *Public Debate under Amadou Toumani Touré.* Retrieved June 09, 2014, from Cultural Anthropology Online: http://www.culanth.org/fieldsights/310-public-debate-under-amadou-toumani-toure

Kaplan, R. D. (2012, April 11). *Africa's Tuareg Dilemma.* Retrieved June 09, 2014, from Stratfor: http://www.stratfor.com/weekly/africas-tuareg-dilemma#axzz3DLWsVj5U

Keen, D. (2012). Greed and grievance in civil war. *The Royal Institute for International Affairs;Chatham House.*

Keita, K. (1998). *Conflict and Conflict resolution in the Sahel: The Tuareg Insurgency in Mali.* Strategic Studies Institute Report: US Army.

Kheir, A. (2010, January 28). *Why the nation-state is wrong for Africa.* Retrieved May 21, 2014, from Pamabazuka News: http://www.pambazuka.net/en/category/comment/61829

Lacher, W. (2012, September 14). *Northern Mali: Key is Strengthening Bamako; ECOWAS Plan Harbors Risks.* Retrieved July 06, 2014, from Global Observatory: http://theglobalobservatory.org/analysis/349-northern-mali-key-is-strengthening-bamako-ecowas-plan-harbors-risks.html

Lacher, W. (2012, September 13). *Organized Crime and Conflict in the Sahel-Sahara Region.* Retrieved July 08, 2014, from Carnegie Endowment : http://carnegieendowment.org/2012/09/13/organized-crime-and-conflict-in-sahel-sahara-region

Lacher, W., & M.Tull, D. (2013). *Mali: Beyond Counterterrorism.* Stiftung Wissenschaft und Politik.

Lath, S. (2012, June 02). *Agression du president Dioncounda Traoré : Oumar Mariko est-il au-dessus de la loi ?* Retrieved June 22, 2014, from Mali Actu / Le Combat: http://maliactu.net/agression-du-president-dioncounda-traore-oumar-mariko-est-il-au-dessus-de-la-loi/#sthash.5VOISzrN.dpuf

Lath, S. (2012, November 29). *Report des concertations nationales: LA COPAM perd le fil conducteur.* Retrieved June 22, 2014, from Mali Web/ Le Combat: http://www.maliweb.net/politique/report-des-concertations-nationales-la-copam-perd-le-fil-conducteur-108596.html

Lecocq, B. (2004). Unemployed intellectuals in the Sahara: The Teshumara nationalist movement and the revolutions in Tuareg society. *INTERNATIONAL REVIEW OF SOCIAL HISTORY*, 87-109.

Lecocq, B. (2005). The bellah question: slave emancipation, race and social categories in late twentieth-century northern Mali. *CANADIAN JOURNAL OF AFRICAN STUDIES*, 42 - 67.

Lecocq, B. (2010). *Disputed Desert. Decolonisation, Competing Nationalisms and Tuareg Rebellions in Northern Mali.* Leiden: Brill.

Lecocq, B. (2010). *Disputed Desert: Decolonisation, Competing Nationalisms and Tuareg Rebellions in Northern Mali.* Brill.

Lecocq, B. (2012, April 05). *Northern Mali: The Things We Assume.* Retrieved March 14, 2014, from e-International Relations: http://www.e-ir.info/2012/04/05/northern-mali-the-things-we-assume/

Lecocq, B. (2013). Mali: this is only the beginning. *Georgetown Journal of International Affairs*, 59 - 69.

Lecocq, B., & Belalimat, N. (2012). The Tuareg: between armed uprising and drought. *Royal African Society*.

Lecocq, B., Mann, G., Whitehouse, B., Badi, D., Pelckmans, L., Belalimat, N., et al. (2013). One Hippopotamus and Eight Blind Analysts: A ultivocal analysis of the 2012 political crisis in the divided Republic of Mali. *Review of African Political Economy*.

Ledoux, H. (2013, January 29). *A Kidal, quel jeu joue le MNLA ?* Retrieved June 22, 2014, from CORENS: http://revuedepressecorens.wordpress.com/2013/01/29/a-kidal-quel-jeu-joue-le-mnla/

Leibow, N. (2013, May 02). *U.N. Peacekeeping Mission in Mali Poised for Failure*. Retrieved July 07, 2014, from The Daily Signal: http://dailysignal.com/2013/05/02/u-n-peacekeeping-mission-in-mali-poised-for-failure/

Levine, M. (2012, September 14). *The Awful Blowback of Benghazi No One Will Learn From*. Retrieved March 18, 2014, from The World Post: http://www.huffingtonpost.com/mark-levine/the-awful-blowback-of-ben_b_1881490.html

LeVine, M. (2013, January 19). *France in Mali: The longue durée of imperial blowback*. Retrieved March 17, 2014, from AlJazeera: http://www.aljazeera.com/indepth/opinion/2013/01/2013119153558185275.html

LeVine, M. (2013, January 19). *France in Mali: The longue durée of imperial blowback*. Retrieved June 08, 2014, from AlJazeera: http://www.aljazeera.com/indepth/opinion/2013/01/2013119153558185275.html

Lewis, D. (2012, April 24). *Analysis: Mali: from democracy poster child to broken state*. Retrieved June 09, 2014, from Reuters: http://www.reuters.com/article/2012/04/24/us-mali-idUSBRE83N09Q20120424

Lister, T. (2013, January 17). *Six reasons events in Mali matter*. Retrieved June 08, 2014, from CNN World: http://www.cnn.com/2013/01/16/world/africa/mali-six-reasons/

Liu, J. (2012, April 24). *Wikipedia, Azawad, and the Art of Internet Statecraft*. Retrieved June 08, 2014, from Vice: http://www.vice.com/en_ca/read/how-azawad-took-to-wikipedia-for-legitimacy

Lussato, C., & Halifa-Legrand, S. (2011, September 17). *La Françafrique, mode d'emploi*. Retrieved June 09, 2014, from Le Nouvel Observateur: http://tempsreel.nouvelobs.com/monde/20110915.OBS0438/la-francafrique-mode-d-emploi.html

Mahjar-Barducci, A. (2012, July 31). *Fighting al-Qaeda for a Secular State near Mali*. Retrieved May 08, 2014, from Gatestone Institute: http://www.gatestoneinstitute.org/3227/azawad-al-qaeda

Mahjar-Barducci, A. (2012, October 24). *MNLA Reaction To ECOWAS Intervention Plan In Azawad: 'We Are The Only Credible Ally In The Fight Against Terrorism In The Sahel'*. Retrieved May 08http://www.memri.org/report/en/0/0/0/0/273/0/6769.htm, 2014, from The Middle East Media Research Institute .

Mali: Islamist Armed Groups Spread Fear in North. (2012, September 25). Retrieved June 05, 2014, from Human Rights Watch: http://www.hrw.org/news/2012/09/25/mali-islamist-armed-groups-spread-fear-north

Mandraud, I. (2012, April 18). *Nina Wallet Intalou, la pasionaria indépendantiste des Touareg maliens*. Retrieved June 08, 2014, from Le Monde: http://www.lemonde.fr/afrique/article/2012/04/18/la-pasionaria-independantiste-des-touareg-maliens_1687042_3212.html

Mann, G. (2012, July 24). *Africanistan? Not Exactly*. Retrieved June 04, 2014, from Freign Policy: http://www.foreignpolicy.com/articles/2012/07/24/africanistan_not_exactly

Mann, G. (2012, December 11). *Mali Prime Minister's resignation edges the Country closer to war*. Retrieved March 13, 2014, from Columbia University Institute of African Studies: http://www.ias.columbia.edu/other-african-election-frances-first-round

Mann, G. (2012, October 17). *Mali: Military Intervention Is Necessary, Inevitable But (Until Now) Impossible*. Retrieved March 13, 2014, from Columbia University Institute of African Studies: http://www.ias.columbia.edu/blog/mali-military-intervention-necessary-inevitable-until-now-impossible

Mann, G. (2012, April 05). *The Mess in Mali*. Retrieved March 14, 2014, from Columbia University Institute of African Studies: http://www.ias.columbia.edu/blog/mess-mali

Mann, M. (1984). *The Autonomous Power of the State: Its Origins, Mechanisms and Results*. Archives européenes de sociologie;.

Mann, M. (2012). *The Sources of Social Power: Volume 2, The Rise of Classes and Nation-States, 1760-1914*. Cambridge.

Marchal, R. (2012). Is a military intervention in Mali unavoidable? *Norwegian Peacebuilding Resource Centre*.

Marchal, R. (2012). The coup in Mali: the result of a long-term crisis or spillover from the Libyan civil war? *Norwegian Peacebuilding Resource Centre*.

Marchal, R. (2012). The reshaping of West Africa after Mu'ammar Qaddafi's fall. *Norwegian Peacebuilding Resource Centre*.

Marchal, R. (2013). Le Sahel dans la crise malienne. *SciencePo*.

Marchal, R. (2013). Mali: Visions of War. *International Journal of Security, Stability and Development*.

Marchal, R. (2013). Military (Mis)Adventures In Mali. *Oxford Journals on African Affairs*.

Mbembe, A. (1992). Provisional Notes on the Postcolony. *Cambridge University Press*, 3-37.

Melly, P., & Darracq, V. (2013). A New Way to Engage? French Policy in Africa from Sarkozy to Hollande. *Chatham House, The Royal Institute of International Affairs* .

Miller, W. (2013, December 26). *Unsustainable Peace in Mali.* Retrieved March 14, 2014, from Georgetown Security Studies Review (GSSR): http://georgetownsecuritystudiesreview.org/2013/12/26/mali-unsustainable-peace/

MNLAMOV. (2012, April 06). *Déclaration d'indépendance de l'Azawad.* Retrieved June 09, 2014, from mnlamov: http://www.mnlamov.net/index.php?view=article&id=169:declaration-dindependance-de-lazawad&tmpl=component&print=1&layout=default&page

Morgan, A. (2012, February 06). *The Causes of the Uprising in Northern Mali.* Retrieved June 02, 2014, from Think Africa Press: http://http://thinkafricapress.com/mali/causes-uprising-northern-mali-tuareg.com/mali/causes-uprising-northern-mali-tuareg

Moyo, D. (2010). *Dead Aid: Why Aid Is Not Working and How There Is a Better Way for Africa.* Douglas & Mcintyre; 1 Reprint edition .

Mrkvicka, K. (2013, December 19). *Intervention in Somalia: A Misguided Model for Success in Mali.* Retrieved July 12, 2014, from Georgetown Security Studies Review (GSSR) : http://georgetownsecuritystudiesreview.org/2013/12/19/intervention-in-somalia-a-misguided-model-for-success-in-mali/

Nanga, J. (2013, February 18). *Une intervention néocoloniale sous leadership français ?* Retrieved June 04, 2014, from Africa Diligence: http://www.africadiligence.com/une-intervention-neocoloniale-sous-leadership-francais-par-jean-nanga/

Neumayer, E., & Plumper, T. (2009). International Terrorism and the Clash of Civilizations. *British journal of political science*, 711-734.

Nicholson, J. B. (2013, January 11). *Can ECOWAS replicate the success of AMISOM in Mali?* Retrieved July 07, 2014, from Small Wars Journal : http://smallwarsjournal.com/blog/can-ecowas-replicate-the-success-of-amisom-in-mali

Nossiter, A. (2012, February 05). *Qaddafi's Weapons, Taken by Old Allies, Reinvigorate an Insurgent Army in Mali.* Retrieved June 05, 2014, from The New York Times: http://www.nytimes.com/2012/02/06/world/africa/tuaregs-use-qaddafis-arms-for-rebellion-in-mali.html?pagewanted=all&_r=0

Palus, N. (2012, June 24). *Islamist Militants in Northern Mali Mix Punishment, Charity.* Retrieved June 04, 2014, from VOA : http://www.voanews.com/content/islamist-militants-in-northern-mali-mix-punishment-charity/1246643.html

Penney, J. (2013, February 08). *Mali's Model Democracy Myth.* Retrieved March 21, 2014, from Think Africa Press: http://thinkafricapress.com/mali/restoring-democracy-mali-never-had

Ping, J. (2014, March 22). *The Crisis in Mali*. Retrieved June 23, 2014, from Harvard International Review: http://hir.harvard.edu/archives/6033

Reuters. (2012, February 09). *Malian rebels seize key border town, civilians flee*. Retrieved June 06, 2014, from Reuters: http://af.reuters.com/article/maliNews/idAFL5E8D8A0G20120209

RFI. (2012, June 11). *Hollande says risk of terrorist groups setting up in Northern Mali*. Retrieved June 04, 2014, from RFI: http://www.english.rfi.fr/africa/20120611-hollande-says-risk-terrorist-groups-setting-northern-mali

RFI. (2012, March 30). *La ville de Kidal, dans le nord du Mali, prise par les rebelles*. Retrieved June 09, 2014, from RFI: http://www.rfi.fr/afrique/20120330-ville-kidal-le-nord-mali-prise-rebelles/

RFI. (2012, March 12). *La ville de Tessalit, au nord du Mali, est aux mains des rebelles du MNLA*. Retrieved May 06, 2014, from RFI: http://www.rfi.fr/afrique/20120312-nord-mali-ville-tessalit-rebelles-mnla-touaregs/

Riondel, L. (2013, March 08). *Algerian authorities annoyed by success of operation "Serval" in northern Mali*. Retrieved June 21, 2014, from Morocco World News: http://www.moroccoworldnews.com/2013/03/81425/algerian-authorities-annoyed-by-success-of-operation-serval-in-northern-mali/?print=pdf

Robert, D., & Heuer, C. (2013). *All That Glitters Is Not Gold: Presidential and Parliamentary* . Retrieved June 08, 2014, from Konrad-Adenauer-Stiftung: http://www.kas.de/wf/doc/kas_11377-544-2-30.pdf?070712125359

Rotberg, R. I. (2003). *When States Fail: Causes and Consequences*. Princeton University Press.

Roy, O. (2013, February 04). *Les raisons de l'engagement de la France au Mali*. Retrieved June 22, 2014, from Le Monde: http://www.lemonde.fr/idees/article/2013/02/04/les-raisons-de-l-engagement-de-la-france-au-mali_1826782_3232.html

Sadatchy, P. (2013). Mali, un dialogue de sourds ? Les suites de l'Accord préliminaire de Ouagadougou. *GROUPE DE RECHERCHE ET D'INFORMATION SUR LA PAIX ET LA SÉCURITÉ*.

Said, E. W. (2001, October 22). *The Clash of Ignorance*. Retrieved May 22, 2014, from The Nation: http://www.thenation.com/article/clash-ignorance#

Sambe, B. (2012, August 30). *La CEDEAO pourra-t-elle parvenir au règlement de la crise malienne* . Retrieved June 09, 2014, from Islam, Societe, Diversite, Universalite: http://bakarysambe.unblog.fr/2012/08/30/la-cedeao-pourra-t-elle-parvenir-au-reglement-de-la-crise-malienne/

Sana, E. (2013, February 25). « *Nous, les soldats maliens, sommes des morts-vivants* ». Retrieved May 09, 2014, from BastaMag: http://www.bastamag.net/Nous-les-soldats-maliens-sommes

Sandor, A. (2013, January 23). *The Problems and Prospects for ECOWAS Intervention in Mali*. Retrieved March 14, 2014, from Africa Portal:

http://www.africaportal.org/articles/2013/01/23/problems-and-prospects-ecowas-intervention-mali

Sandor, A. (2013, January 23). *The Problems and Prospects for ECOWAS Intervention in Mali.* Retrieved July 05, 2014, from Africa Portal: http://www.africaportal.org/articles/2013/01/23/problems-and-prospects-ecowas-intervention-mali

Schmitz, G. P. (2014, January 21). *Europe's Sole Military Force: Giving France Respect Where It Is Due.* Retrieved June 21, 2014, from Spiegel International: http://www.spiegel.de/international/europe/as-the-sole-strategic-force-in-europe-france-deserves-respect-a-944693.html

Schneider, J. (2013, February 01). *Editor's Q & A: What's the Deal with Mali?* Retrieved June 07, 2014, from Think Africa Press: http://thinkafricapress.com/mali/editors-q-whats-deal-mali

Soares, U. (2012, November 14). *Opération militaire au Mali : la France n'interviendra pas «elle-même».* Retrieved June 08, 2014, from RFI: http://www.rfi.fr/afrique/20121113-operation-militaire-mali-france-interviendra-pas-elle-meme-union-africaine-addis-abeba-conseil-securite/

Sow, A. (2013). Memoirs, religion and morality in Mali's national memory. *The Sohaib and Sara Abbasi Program in Islamic Studies.*

Sow, O. (2008, March 27). *Bè b'i ba bolo: La leçon de morale.* Retrieved June 08, 2014, from Mali Web: http://www.maliweb.net/category.php?NID=28843

Sow, Y. (2014, June 16). *Révélations troublantes contre la France : les balles du fusil Famas extraites des militaires maliens blessés à Kidal.* Retrieved June 22, 2014, from MaliWeb/ L'Inter de Bamako: http://www.maliweb.net/armee/revelations-troublantes-contre-france-les-balles-du-fusil-famas-extraites-militaires-maliens-blesses-kidal-368952.html

Soysa, I. d. (2001). Paradise Is a Bazaar? Greed, Creed, and Governance in Civil War, 1989–99*. *Journal of Peace and Research*, 395–416.

Sphinx, L. (2007). *ATT-cratie: la promotion d'un homme et de son clan.* Harmattan.

Stewart, F. (2010). *Horizontal Inequalities as a Cause of Conflict: A Review of CRISE Findings.* Centre for Research on Inequality, Human Security and Ethnicity(CRISE).

Strategy Page. (2012, March 08). *Logistics: American Robots Sustain The Siege of Tessalit.* Retrieved May 06, 2014, from Strategy Page: http://www.strategypage.com/htmw/htlog/articles/20120308.aspx

Sylla, C. (2012, April 09). *Mali's coup leader sits down with the country's future president, will hand over power* . Retrieved June 23, 2014, from AFP: http://news.nationalpost.com/2012/04/09/malis-coup-leader-sits-down-with-the-countrys-future-president-will-hand-over-power/

The Moor Next Door. (2012, June 10). *RE: Canard Enchaîné, Qatar in northern Mali and Algeria.* Retrieved June 15, 2014, from The Moor Next Door: http://themoornextdoor.wordpress.com/2012/06/10/re-canard-enchaine-qatar-in-northern-mali-and-algeria/

Theroux-Benoni, L.-A. (2013, April 22). *Lessons from the Malian Crisis for the International Security Architecture.* Retrieved March 23, 2014, from ISNBLOG: http://isnblog.ethz.ch/international-relations/lessons-from-the-malian-crisis-for-the-international-security-architecture

Theroux-Benoni, L.-A. (2013, January 15). *Mali conflict going global.* Retrieved March 23, 2014, from The Voice of Russia: http://voiceofrussia.com/2013_01_15/Mali-conflict-going-global/

Théroux-Bénoni, L.-A. (2013). Mali in the aftermath of the French military intervention / Le Mali au lendemain de de l'operation militaire francaise. *ISS* .

Théroux-Bénoni, L.-A. (2013, December). *Mali: Making Peace while Preparing for War.* Retrieved May 25, 2014, from Prezi: http://prezi.com/2qdrgzyfxyzi/mali-making-peace-while-preparing-for-war/

Théroux-Bénoni, L.-A., & Zounmenou, D. (2012). Mali: Making Peace While Preparing for War. *ISS ECOWAS Peace and Security Report.*

Thiam, A. (2011, August 10). *Mali : ATT lance sa stratégie anti-Aqmi de développement du nord.* Retrieved June 08, 2014, from Jeune Afrique: http://www.jeuneafrique.com/Article/ARTJAWEB20110810085636/algerie-france-canada-developpement-mali-mali-att-lance-sa-strategie-anti-aqmi-de-developpement-du-nord.html

Thurston, A. (2013, May 14). *Somalia, Mali, and the Weakness of Analogical Thinking.* Retrieved July 13, 2014, from Sahel Blog: http://sahelblog.wordpress.com/2013/05/14/somalia-mali-and-the-weakness-of-analogical-thinking/

Thurston, A., & Lebovich, A. (2013). A Handbook on Mali's 2012-2013 Crisis. *Institute for the Study of Islamic Thought in Africa (ISITA).*

Tilly, C. (1975). *The Formation of National States in Western Europe.* Princeton University.

Tine, L. (2012, November 26). *Crise Au Mali – Pourquoi Une Intervention Militaire Est-Elle Nécessaire?* Retrieved June 02, 2014, from Le Congolais: http://www.lecongolais.cd/crise-au-mali-pourquoi-une-intervention-militaire-est-elle-necessaire/

Tinti, P. (2012, October 05). *Understanding Algeria's Northern Mali Policy.* Retrieved June 23, 2014, from Think Africa Press: http://thinkafricapress.com/mali/understanding-algeria-northern-mali-aqim-mujao-ansar-dine

Touchard, L. (2012, October 16). *Intervention au Mali : dans quelques mois ou "quelques semaines" ?* Retrieved June 23, 2014, from Jeune Afrique: http://www.jeuneafrique.com/Article/ARTJAWEB20121016180631/

Touchard, L. (2013, jUNE 18). *Armée malienne : le difficile inventaire*. Retrieved June 12, 2014, from Jeune Afrique: http://www.jeuneafrique.com/Article/ARTJAWEB20130618120951/

Touchard, L. (2014, January 10). *Mali - Serval : la France a-t-elle piégé les jihadistes en janvier 2013 ?* Retrieved June 12, 2014, from Jeune Afrique: http://www.jeuneafrique.com/Article/ARTJAWEB20140109170210/

Touchard, L. (2014, January 30). *Mali : retour sur la bataille décisive de Konna*. Retrieved June 12, 2014, from Jeune Afrique: http://www.jeuneafrique.com/Article/ARTJAWEB20140130165338/

Traub, J. (2012, April 13). *Two Cheers for Malian Democracy*. Retrieved June 09, 2014, from Foreign Policy: http://www.foreignpolicy.com/articles/2012/04/13/two_cheers_for_malian_democracy

Uchenna, O. (2012). Epistemological Foundations Of Nation Building: The Paradigm Of Postcolonial Africa. *Annales Philosophici; Issue 4*.

UNSC. (2012). *Security Council Calls For 'Road Map' For Restoration Of Constitutional Order In Mali, Unanimously Adopting Resolution 2056 (2012)*. United Nations Security Council.

UNSC. (2013). *Report of the Secretary-General on the situation in Mali* . United Nations Security Council .

Védrines, A. (2012, July 11). *Les sympathisants du MNLA redoutent un « génocide » contre les Touaregs*. Retrieved May 08, 2014, from Slate Afrique: http://blog.slateafrique.com/maligraphe/2012/11/07/les-sympathisants-du-mnla-redoutent-un-genocide-contre-les-touaregs/

Vines, A. (2013). *A decade of African Peace and Security Architecture*. Chatham House, The Royal Institute of International Affairs .

Vogt, M., & Muyangwa, M. (2000). An Assessment of the OAU Mechanism for Conflict Prevention, Management, and Resolution, 1993-2000. *International Peace Institute*.

Weber, M. (1946). *Politics as a Vocation*. New York: Gerth and Mills.

Weiss, T. G., & Welz, M. (2014). *The UN and the African Union in Mali and beyond: a shotgun wedding?* Chatham House, The Royal Institute of International Affairs.

Whitehouse, B. (2012, August 30). *What went wrong in Mali?* Retrieved March 14, 2014, from London Review of Books: http://www.lrb.co.uk/v34/n16/bruce-whitehouse/what-went-wrong-in-mali

Wilandh, H. (2012, November 26). *Wrong paths to peace: the re-emergence of armed violence in northern Mali*. Retrieved June 05, 2014, from Stockholm International Peace Research Institute: http://www.sipri.org/media/newsletter/essay/Wilandh_Nov12

Wing, S. D. (2013, April 19). *Mali's Precarious Democracy and the Causes of Conflict.* Retrieved June 09, 2014, from United States Institute of Peace : http://www.usip.org/publications/mali-s-precarious-democracy-and-the-causes-of-conflict

Wyss, M. (2013). The Gendarme Stays in Africa: France's Military Role in Côte d'Ivoire. *African Conflict & Peacebuilding Review* , 81-111.

Yalkoué, B. (2013, February 08). *Amnistie-amnistie : Le crépuscule des putschistes ?* Retrieved April 23, 2014, from Mali Web: http://www.maliweb.net/armee/amnistie-amnistie-le-crepuscule-des-putschistes-125991.html

Yalkoué, B. (2014, January 20). *Coopération militaire Mali- France : 21 janvier 1961- 11 janvier 2013 : Retrait contraignant, retour en liesse des enjeux politiques trahissent le Mali.* Retrieved March 23, 2014, from Mali Actu: http://maliactu.info/crise-malienne/cooperation-militaire-mali-france-21-janvier-1961-11-janvier-2013-retrait-contraignant-retour-en-liesse-des-enjeux-politiques-trahissent-le-mali

Zyck, S., & Muggah, R. (2013). *Conflicts Colliding in Mali and the Sahel.* Retrieved May 15, 2014, from International Journal for Stability, Security and Development: http://www.stabilityjournal.org/article/view/sta.bf/72

Lightning Source UK Ltd.
Milton Keynes UK
UKHW01f0610060918
328419UK00001B/223/P